The American Paradise Series

ABBA GERASIM
AND HIS LETTERS TO HIS BROTHERHOOD

Father Gerasim in front of his cell
during summertime, expecting guests for tea.

Abba Gerasim

And His Letters to His Brotherhood

(TO ABBOT HERMAN, 1961–1966)

New Valaam Monastery
ST. HERMAN OF ALASKA BROTHERHOOD
Spruce Island, Alaska 1998

Copyright 1998 by the
St. Herman of Alaska Brotherhood

Address all correspondence to:
St. Herman of Alaska Brotherhood
P.O. Box 70
Platina, California 96076

and

New Valaam Monastery
P.O. Box 90
Ouzinkie, Alaska 99644

Cover: Archimandrite Gerasim (✝1969), hermit of "New Valaam," Spruce Island, Alaska. *Courtesy of Kodiak Historical Society.*

Library of Congress Cataloging in Publication Data

Schmaltz, Gerasim, Father (1888-1969)
  Abba Gerasim and his letters to his brotherhood
  Translated from the Russian

Library of Congress Catalogue Card Number: 98-84480

ISBN 0-938635-82-4

DEDICATED

WITH GRATITUDE TO ARCHIMANDRITE GERASIM'S
FORMER SPIRITUAL CHILDREN OF SPRUCE ISLAND,
WHO ON THEIR ISLAND USED TO GUARD
ST. HERMAN'S RELICS AND MONASTIC BROTHERHOOD.

Archimandrite Gerasim near the chapel of Sts. Sergius and Herman, over the grave of St. Herman, in the 1950's.

CONTENTS

Archimandrite Gerasim near his flower garden.

INTRODUCTION

... The nameday of Father Gerasim. May the Lord grant his soul repose. A scary thought deeply pangs my soul: that our Brotherhood has inherited precisely his state. We are hated on one side, and not understood by our own people on the other. O Lord, the loneliness is frightening. But we have St. Herman, who rises sharply against the background of the dark sea roaring with worldliness. Save us, O holy Father Herman, your servants.

Chronicle of the St. Herman Brotherhood
March 4/17, 1972
Platina, California

I AM SITTING in a *barabara* facing the roaring ocean. Beneath me spreads the swampy field—now thickly closed in by ice and snow— where years ago St. Herman's hamlet was located, a little community of Aleut orphans whom he gathered and cared for.

For a century this spot was abandoned. St. Herman's chapel of the Meeting of the Lord, which once had stood here, was not to be seen. That little chapel had a bell which St. Herman had requested of the mighty governor Wrangell, the chief of the Russian-American colonies. Wrangell built the chapel for St. Herman, giving over the whole of the east side of Spruce Island to New Valaam Monastery and making St. Herman in charge of it, like an abbot. This is the very spot where I sit now and think of how it must have been in 1834, when Baron Ferdinand Wrangell with his wife and a whole entourage visited little "Appa" (Father) Herman, as the Aleuts used to call him. Wrangell's "deeding" of the land turned out to be a prophetic document, for no one else settled this area, which is still called Monks' Lagoon, leaving it truly for monastic solitude.

A hundred years elapsed before another monk (a monk similar to St. Herman, as the Saint himself had prophesied) came from the Kaluga area of Holy Russia to settle here. He settled a bit further into the spruce forest, right next to the very barabara where St. Herman had lived alone in seclusion and had died amidst divine fragrance, to the sobbing of his once-again-orphaned, defenseless, scared little Aleut children. This newcomer was from St. Tikhon of Kaluga Monastery, where St. Herman's disciple, Schemamonk Sergius Yanovsky, had eventually become a schemamonk and died. The monk's name was Father Gerasim, and we want to present him here in his true light.

Fr. Archimandrite Gerasim first visited St. Herman's grave in 1927, and upon a prayer to the Saint was surrounded by an aromatic fragrance of paradisal origin. Surprised and in awe, he asked the Saint to allow him to come and settle here, to guard his grave and his hermitage, "when the time will come." And less than a decade later, being persecuted by the Kodiak clergy just as was St. Herman, Fr. Gerasim fled to Spruce Island, being fortified with heroic fearlessness. He came soon after seeing a vision of St. Herman face to face, ringing paschal bells and inviting him to live and guard his "New Valaam" monastic heritage. Fr. Gerasim lived there all alone for thirty years, abandoned and slandered by the powerful "official clerics" of anti-monastic sentiment, modeling his lifestyle on what he learned in his Optina-inspired St. Tikhon's Hermitage and his beloved Mount Athos, which he had visited in his youth.

Fr. Gerasim left an abundance of letters, which serve as a veritable testament of his solitary life in the deserted New Valaam Monastery and his stoic stand at the post of Orthodox monastic concerns of the 20th century. These letters remain now as a document—almost as a chronicle of the severe ascetic life of a desert dweller, although they were never intended to be such. In actuality, they were written in moments of despair and abandonment, when, in order to fight the eternal foe of monks, Fr. Gerasim poured out his soul on paper to his father-confessor, Archimandrite Ambrose of Canada, and to his close friends: Abbots John and Nicholas of Mount Athos, and Panteleimon of Jordanville; Bishops Tikhon and Mark of San Francisco; Archimandrites Vladimir and Constantine; his closest Michael Z. Vinokouroff (with whom he formed 600 pages of mutual correspondence); the famous writer Boris Zaitseff; and myself, the youngest of them all. In writing these letters, he relieved the tension of his solitary battle to retain sanity in the intense wilderness, cold, and horrid weather of these northern jungles and tundra, which are similar in intensity to the abodes of the great ascetics of Siberia in recent centuries. In addition to the letters, he wrote short articles and memoirs of Tsarist Russia for various spiritual magazines and newspapers.

When I visited Fr. Gerasim just eight years before his death, I encountered, to my great surprise, a living relic of the past glory of the Orthodox monastic flowering which had occurred at the turn of this century. He was full of vigor and genuine monastic inspiration, which all his letters, as I read them later, do not convey. In fact, these "ramblings" of a seemingly embittered old man do not give due credit to his true spirit, which I beheld that summer of 1961. At that time he told me a whole fascinating array of stories gathered from his rich life's experience, which reflected the sobriety and vigor of a valiant hero who was overcoming millions of spiritual attacks by the enemy of our salvation, a deeply spiritual "knower" of the mechanism of the human heart, and a man of prayer. I recorded then just bits and pieces, and was not able to fathom the whole breadth and depth of the man whom I faced. I was too unprepared, and my nine-day meeting with him was the one and only.

I managed, however, to develop a rapport with his soul's tenor, and we corresponded almost to the very end of his life. These letters I preserved, and although they do not show the essence of his soul's disposition and its real make-up, they nevertheless show his world, his values, and his aspirations. In reading them, one must keep in mind that they were written as an antidote to despair, hopelessness, and bitter defeats. When his patience would run out, he would write. His letters were gropings and searching for relief, when he resorted to the little comfort he could draw from his colorful memory, being surrounded by the loneliness of howling blizzards and the roaring, breaking ocean, in which all hell broke loose.

Fr. Gerasim invited me to stay with him and to continue his stand. With his blessing I eventually managed to create a little group of young monastic zealots and brought part of them to the shores of Monks' Lagoon to revive St. Herman's New Valaam Monastery. We settled in Fr. Gerasim's vacant cell as if it had been waiting for us all these long years: waiting for our arrival, for after his death there had not been a single monastic aspirant to suffer for Christ in this intensely lonely place. With God's help we built a little chapel on the spot where perhaps stood that chapel built by the order of the chief of the whole of the Russian- American colonies, Ferdinand Wrangell, and we even hung a small clanking bell, for both the chapel and the bells were gone long before Fr. Gerasim's arrival in 1927.

Now for the last fifteen years we have revived monastic life on Spruce Island, and Monks' Lagoon is again having the daily cycle of monastic services in the way St. Herman used to have them: according to the Valaam rule. We pray in a frescoed little chapel, while ringing St. Herman's bells.

Once again the monastic hamlet is alive. And to the inhabitants of these humble premises, washed by the waves and swells of the mighty ocean, we have now an echo of Fr. Gerasim's letters, written to me as a living legacy coming from the pen of a man who was chosen by St. Herman himself to revive his monastic "heavenly abode." Once St. Herman took a child and, addressing him, said, "On this spot there will be a monastery in time." This now, to some small measure, has come to pass on Monks' Lagoon, alas, evoking envy and hatred in those who do not live according to God's law of love.

INTRODUCTION

Let these humble letters, bequeathed to my monks as their own inheritance, be to them a witness of a monastic, uncompromising stand in Truth before the secularizing apostate world, which is engulfing even the Orthodox Church. The letters are a testimony of the power and glory of Holy Russia—whose eternal echo is so well recorded in the grieving soul of our founder, Archimandrite Gerasim—and are a source of inspiration for "his" monks to continue their personal spiritual growth. May that growth increase and touch the souls of the new "orphans of St. Herman," the Aleuts, to come to join the monastic ranks of New Valaam in Alaska.

What was the source of Fr. Gerasim's power of endurance and his stand, so erect before the Lord, when hundreds of monastics of his time fell away and disappeared? It was his inner happiness, born of the memory of otherworldliness imprinted in his soul, which carried him across the depth of the stormy sea of life and its mishaps and dangers. This inner warmth cannot but touch living souls who have not yet lost their Godliness

Fr. Gerasim's vision—alas, barely accentuated in his correspondence with me—was based on his guarding of the inner eye of genuine hesychastic experience, in which he trained himself well during his formative years.

This is my wish, that all of us who have been enriched by Fr. Gerasim's touching spiritual presence will bring forth spiritual fruit, will not be barren, but will, while we still have time, develop that "inward eye which is a bliss of solitude," as a poet used to say. For solitude, the Fathers say, is the ladder by means of which even sinners ascend to heaven.

... It is snowing hard now. Soon it will be Christmas Eve, and we shall gather, glorifying the newborn Savior in our warm little chapel, and shall ring the Christmas bells to our hearts' content.

And St. Herman will hear and bless us.

God bless us everyone.

Abbot Herman, Christmas Eve, 1996

"It is I who am ringing the Paschal bells! ... Batiushka, don't be sad!" Thus spoke St. Herman to Archimandrite Gerasim in a vision, after which the latter settled on New Valaam (Spruce Island, Alaska) for good.
Iconographic painting by Br. Gleb, 1961.

✳

BELLS AND DOMES AT MONKS' LAGOON

On Monks' Lagoon on East Spruce Island,
Washed by the ever-changing tides and swells,
God-chosen monks give vows of silence,
While angels sing and ring celestial bells.

> Monastic hamlet, Valaam the new,
> Where Appa Herman was inquired to tell
> Their needs: Perhaps the chapel to renew?
> He said: "If only we could have a bell!"

And that was done, confirmed with sealed decrees,
Monastic life to thrive amidst sea swells
Oblivious of time. But in a hundred years
The chapel's gone, no trace of singing bells.

> But he's alive in hallowed radiance there,
> Attracting monks to his abandoned cells,
> Where, wrapped in purity of fragrant air,
> They see him face to face ring Paschal bells.

Then seven monks arrived upon that shore
At Appa's and Gerasim's invitation,
Monastic life once more there to restore
And be for others inspiration.

To build a chapel they towed wood
Across the sea, rainbow in sight,
And spouting whales, as if they understood,
While hail in May fell down to their delight.

Atop Monk's Rock the eagles gaze
How Paschal joy will resurrect
Appa's new chapel for new days,
Old Valaam there to reflect.

And cut off by the ocean foams
Of boisterous storms, in earthen cells,
Monks live to see there golden domes,
While ringing their triumphant bells.

Ring out, serene celestial bells!
Proclaim Christ's Birth and Resurrection,
Against majestic waves and swells
Ring out to God for His protection.

On Monks' Lagoon, on East Spruce Island,
Washed by the ever-changing tides and swells,
God-chosen monks give vows of silence,
While angels sing and ring celestial bells.

Christmas, 1996
Monks' Lagoon, New Valaam

The Autobiography of Fr. Gerasim

Through His Correspondence

With love and great respect I greet you now—
For draughts of work and prayer you have drunk.
I have but one desire: I wish somehow
The world will know what is, in truth, a monk.

—Michael Z. Vinokouroff to Fr. Gerasim

Fr. Gerasim as an Afognak parish priest, in his earlier days.

The Autobiography of Fr. Gerasim
Through His Correspondence

*Gathered from letters to many of his friends
scattered throughout the whole world.*

COMMEMORATED SEPTEMBER 30 (†1969)

T HE BLESSED MEMORY of the reviver of monastic life on New
Valaam, Fr. Archimandrite Gerasim, is for American monasticism a link
connecting the fledgling monastic yearning and strivings of modern
America with the powerful monastic army of Holy Russia.

Having received monastic training in the Optina cast, in a monastery located not far from Optina, the St. Tikhon of Kaluga Monastery,
Fr. Gerasim absorbed all of the best it had to offer and brought it with
him to America, when he came as a temporary missionary and was
forced to stay in Alaska because of the revolution. His soul became
immediately inclined towards the poor, abandoned Aleuts; and he
dedicated the rest of his life to them as a missionary-pastor. As a monk
he renewed the monastic tradition of St. Herman on New Valaam.

In the biography presented below, it is clear that St. Herman called
Fr. Gerasim to his New Valaam. But Fr. Gerasim fulfilled that call
when, because of church in-fighting, his eyes were opened to the
foremost Christian duty to be obedient to Christ, Who came to save
sinners from passion, hatred and various human prohibitions and
divisions. Fr. Gerasim's conscience did not allow him to take sides in
the schisms occurring in the church; and for the sake of remaining

faithful to Christ's Church he preferred to flee to the island and to the as-yet-unglorified and abandoned "Lowly Herman"—as the holy elder in his humility called himself.

And Fr. Gerasim was not mistaken. God blessed him to revive the forgotten skete with monastic fervor, and at last to found an active monastery—at once a desert and a missionary outpost—through the brotherhood named after St. Herman in California, in 1963. The Brotherhood, located in Platina, California, is actively publishing the resurrected Russian-language magazine *Russian Pilgrim* and currently works to send thousands of copies to Russia, inspiring the Russian people with its non-partisan message. For now at least, the Lord has granted the Brotherhood the possibility of catechizing throughout the land with the ideal of Holy Russia. Fr. Gerasim's spiritual nearness from the other world is felt by his child-brotherhood in this effort.

In his solitude Fr. Gerasim cried a great deal over Russia, held captive by the cruel atheistic government, and over the falling away from Christian love by Orthodox living in freedom outside of Russia. He wrote to many publications, but much of what he wrote was never published because he in fact did not belong to any particular side of the warring jurisdictions. He only belonged to "Christ's jurisdiction," as he liked to express it.

On his island "amongst the melancholy storms," according to the poet Pushkin's expression, he was a crying, sighing, outcast Russian monk. Just the same, he did not become downcast in spirit, but firmly held on to his spiritual inheritance, literally living and dying by it, and he was in our estimation a true hero. He did not forsake his monastic rule or services, and he generously shared his spiritual world with whomever happened to write him. Thanks to his correspondence he is alive even today. He wrote prolifically, simply and from the heart. Our Brotherhood's archives possess over 300 pages of his letters to various private individuals, published letters to editors, and articles. The following excerpts are only scattered fragments dealing specifically with his biography.

He also corresponded for many years with a friend of his, an archivist of the Library of Congress in Washington, Michael Zinovievich Vinokouroff. A 600-page correspondence arose, showing from Fr. Gerasim's side the tenor of his life in bright colors.* With these autobiographical notes from the letters to Vinokurov, we would like to share with you the image of a Russian monk exiled to a distant land—persecuted by his own clergy and separated from his homeland by the Godless communist government, which had destroyed his dear monastery of St. Tikhon of Kaluga and tortured and killed his monastic brothers, while the American government during those very years officially recognized the Soviet system as the lawful authority over Holy Russia!

Will the world—will young Russia—understand? This is the question of the future. But for young Americans, like Fr. Seraphim Rose who loved him fervently, and for the thousands who now venerate him thanks to the book written about him by the young monk Gerasim, the image of Fr. Gerasim of New Valaam is sacred! May young monastic aspirants be inspired to take up the easy yoke of Christ—of standing for the Truth! May God grant it!

This autobiography was created from his letters to his friends, written over a period of forty years. It is as the cry of the soul of a desert dweller: a cry not just to himself, but addressed to the entire world, though written without any intention of publication. We have noted the date of individual letters at the end of each excerpt.

Abbot Herman
Feast of the Nativity
1991

---

*These letters are now in the Alaskan State Library in Juneau.

The earliest existing picture of Fr. Gerasim as a novice
at St. Tikhon's Monastery in the Kaluga region.

The pre-revolutionary town of Alexin in the year 1913,
from a postcard of that period.

1. Childhood

On October 28, 1888, in the small house of Doctor I. G. Seleznev (in the town of Alexin), Misha, Mishel, Mikhail Alexandrovich Schmaltz came into the world, but from the year 1915, April 25, Monk Gerasim.   [November 10, 1961]

* * *

My father was a sober, honest man, but fate never sort of shined upon his life.   [March 23, 1962]

* * *

My older brother died on December 25, 1905. He died in the morning, at the end of Liturgy. I still remember what a sad time that was for us. He was young, only twenty years old, handsome and curly-haired.   _ [January 28, 1963]

* * *

In Holy Russia, in our time, there were also non-monastic priests of holy life. They served with fear of God, unhurriedly and reverently. And I am fortunate in that I had, during my childhood and youth in our town of Alexin, all five priests who were excellent pastors: sober, honest, faithful. And unmercenary. They served for half a century at single parishes. But after they died, the ones who replaced them were already not the same. But, I must say that everything began to change for us very rapidly. Students who finished seminary would rarely, rarely put on the priest's riassa and did not wish to travel the thorny path.

[November 10, 1940]

* * *

Oh, where are you, my dear Homeland; where are your little houses made of pine logs, with brick ovens? For us, and even for the poor man in his little hut, it was warm and cozy even at 30 degrees below zero.

I had a comrade, Alyosha Pavlov, and we used to run to his house to warm up after sledding in the hills in the terrible cold. Oh, how I loved their little house, where finches and tomtits sang in their cages. Of course there was a holy icon corner, with lampadas. It was peaceful and quiet in their home.

At that time I, the child Misha, only dreamt about monasteries, about a hut built in the woods, and thought: "How I would like to have such a little house-cell, in the woods upon the meadow." And there were many meadows around our town. There was one surrounded by birches, where there was not far away a spring with cold, crystal-clear water. Oh, how I loved that meadow. When I visited it I would plan where I would build a church and a cell. A cell is a tiny wooden house, and not a luxurious palace, as they made in our wealthy monasteries.

Sweet, pure childish dreams. But the dream never left me even when I lived in St. Tikhon's Monastery.   [November 10, 1961]

✻ ✻ ✻

In Russia, Christians venerated the holy Prophet Elias, and he is indeed a wondrous man. Not far from the town of Alexin was a hill called St. Elias Hill. Of course, by the small mounds and by the gravestones, which had all but disappeared into the earth, one could tell that there was a graveyard there. But tradition has it that there was also a church there dedicated to the Prophet Elias. They conducted processions to that hill. In 1813 a small stone chapel was built there. I believe that when the church stood there, it embellished that hill. For the river Oka runs near it, and from the river, to the south, it appears very high and steep. It reminded me of a little piece of Athos. But if trees were to be planted on top and all around and a church were to be built, it would be a wonderful little corner of Holy Russia!

* * *

I often remember the Russian log houses and Russian-style ovens. How nice it was, warm and cozy. It was warm in all the rooms. But at home in Russia we praised what was foreign, thinking that it was something wonderful and different. Lands beyond our borders, Turkey and Greece, I saw in 1911. But no, I did not like it there, with the exception of Athos, with its ancient monasteries and sketes. In 1915 I had to travel through Romania, Bulgaria, Yugoslavia (then Serbia), Italy and Portugal. But my homeland is the nicest country. It is a beautiful and rich country.

It is cold, our winters are long, but they are lovely, especially when the downy frost artistically decorates all the trees, all the brush.

Yes, even our winters are magical.

* * *

When the moon is out, when it shines upon the snowdrifts, the trees bent with frost, it is something wonderful. The snow is transformed into diamonds that flash flames of all the colors of the rainbow.

Here, on islands near the sea, there is not the beauty of Holy Russia in the wintertime.

But soon, soon my heart will cease to beat, to suffer for my homeland, for all that is my own.... [November 10, 1961]

* * *

I have loved the Canon from my youth, and the one who made me love it was a nun from the Tula Dormition Convent. Even now I can as though hear her prayerful wail: "Most holy Mother of God, save us." In monasteries it was read without leaving anything out. And it was read with tenderness of feeling. Also akathists. I do so love them....

[November 14, 1963]

2. Blessed Euphrosyne
(Commemorated July 3, 1855)

It is precisely religious faith in God, faith in the intercessions of the Mother of God and the God-pleasers, that consoles my soul. The Mother of God, Her holy icons—I have loved from early in life. I also love the God-pleasers. I love, venerate and pray also to the fools-for-Christ's sake. This is the highest Christian *podvig*, to crucify one's self for the sake of Christ. Not far from our town of Alexin, three versts away in the village of Koliupanovo, there labored for her salvation Blessed* Euphrosyne (Princess Eudokia of Viazma). In 1955 it was one hundred years since her blessed repose. Her remains, according to the orders of Metropolitan Plato of Moscow, were buried under the church of the Kazan Mother of God. In the church was a memorial stone with an expensive cloth covering.

My grandmothers knew her and visited her. My mother was healed by her when she was dangerously sick with typhus. The old Bishop Philaret Drozdov also respected her, and when she lived in Serpukhov in a convent, he would come and carry on long conversations with her. The village of Koliupanovo sprawls picturesquely along the river Oka, and the view of Alexin from the church is very lovely. She died on the fourth of June, 1855. An "abnormal" person** can not foretell exactly what will happen in the next seventy-five or one-hundred years . Such people were visited even by educated people, by the learned and by people of all classes.

I first heard of Blessed Xenia when I was still a child in the highly provincial town of Alexin, Tula province. Later, when I had become a novice, I learned that this righteous woman was venerated by tens of

---

*Blessed refers to a fool for Christ's sake, which she was. See Appendix II.

** The communists were attacking the clairvoyant fool-for-Christ's-sake, Eldress Euphrosyne, calling her "abnormal," because people flocked to her for comfort.

St. Euphrosyne the "Unknown."
An icon of the newly canonized Fool-for-Christ of Koliupanovo.

thousands of Christian Russians, all across our great Russia. In 1914, when I happened to be in St. Petersburg, I visited her holy grave in the Smolensk Cemetery. A beautiful chapel had been built over it, and it was decorated with good icons. Over her grave hung, if I am not mistaken, over fifty lampadas, many of them are of great value. How good it was to pray there! I visited that chapel three times. Each time I encountered many pilgrims, and each time pannikhidas were being served.   [November 14, 1963]

* * *

I remember how my religious grandmother told my mother about the war of 1812. Then they did not yet have the new Dormition Cathedral. (Among the parishioners of this Cathedral was also the Schmaltz family). People prayed in the ancient cathedral, where the floors were made of white stone slabs. Many people gathered in the ancient cathedral—war and woes humbled all—and everyone hurried to God's church to pray. The priest was deeply religious, and often served molebens for the granting of victory to the Russian army. He read the prayer not from a book, but he himself called to God, asking also for the remission of sins of the Russian Orthodox people and the granting of victory to them over the powerful enemy. Everyone in church cried, the whole church cried! To such an extent they cried that, when they arose on the stone floor there were traces everywhere of human tears! That is how fervently they prayed and repented, our dear ancestors; and the Lord heard their prayer—the enemies of our fatherland were defeated.   [December 1959]

* * *

I remember my childhood, my homeland and the ancient church (St. John the Forerunner), where there were side altars dedicated to the holy Archangel Michael. The church was very old, nearly 500 years. There were old icons in it and old paintings. But it is no more. It was destroyed by barbarians of the 20th century, and in its place they broke out a square and erected a monument to Lenin, but that was destroyed by the Germans. It is obvious that such was God's will. I still have a photograph of the church. I remember that its massive walls were steeped in incense. The head priest, Fr. Alexander Pokrovsky, served there nearly fifty years. He was an excellent priest and served reverently. Alas, you do not meet such priests these days.   [November, 1964]

3. St. Tikhon's Monastery

My youthful dreams of a desert cell never left me, even in St. Tikhon's Monastery. You walk into the woods and spy a beautiful meadow surrounded by fir, pine and birch trees, and you think, "This is where I would build my little house—a cell!" What blessings: greenery, flowers, blue skies and fragrant air.

Then you remember: who would allow you to build a hut? For even though you live in the monastery, it is all monastery property. And with what means would you, a poor youth, build it? Well, there was a time when religious youths would leave for our forests, find a pretty spot and built a hut and a small church. I thought then, "How fortunate they were. Now it is not that way; everything belongs to the public treasury, to landowners and wealthy people."   [1961]

* * *

A rural priest in the Kaluga diocese, out of hatred toward his brother-in-law, committed arson, was caught, tried and exiled to a monastery for the rest of his life without the right to serve, but he was permitted to concelebrate. He lived in St. Tikhon's Monastery, and his matushka lived in the Shamordino Kazan Convent. I visited him in the monastery, and we had discussions. He loved flowers, and his only window was decorated with jars of flowers. He was an excellent, humble elder, Fr. Dimitry. As I recall, no one ever reminded him of his past, nor criticized him—not even coarse, tipsy novices.   [1961]

***

God allows even good people to suffer. This is what some monks in St. Tikhon's Monastery told me. It was during the time of Fr. Archimandrite Moses the Second, "Moses the small," as they called him because of his small stature. But he served very beautifully, his wonderful voice could be heard in every corner of the magnificent cathedral. He was extremely cautious and terribly squeamish.

Well, the riassophore monk Michael Zaitsev's thick hair began to quickly fall out. One of the brothers told Fr. Archimandrite Moses that Fr. Michael had syphilis. Of course, he could have had a doctor examine him rather than believe this gossip. But Fr. Moses, who was such a terribly abrupt man, did not wish to keep such a person in the monastery. He called him in and politely, not mentioning the illness nor the hair, invited him to go to another monastery.

"Yes, this would be better for you." Learning that he had been slandered, the poor monk Michael was very sorrowful. But he did not want to leave his monastery; he was already registered there.

In those times, in the Orlov diocese, there labored a holy priest, Fr. George (of Chekriakov village),* whose fame thundered across all of Russia. Fr. Michael Zaitsev set off for this holy priest for advice. Fr. George received him affectionately, heard him out, and said:

"Let us pray." They both fell on their knees and prayed. When they finished praying, Fr. George took some holy water, sprinkled the monk's head, and said:

"Don't be downcast, father; you are a monk and should remember: without sorrows, there is no salvation." Then he brought out his epitrachelion and, giving it to Fr. Michael, said: "This is for you as a memento, take it!" And Fr. Michael returned to the monastery happy and joyful. Soon his hair grew back, and he was tonsured in the mantle with the name Misail. In July of 1906, when I was on obedience in the

---

*A lay-priest ascetic confessor known for his daring, extreme humility; and a friend of Elder Ambrose of Optina.

General view of St. Tikhon's Monastery, 1907.

Dormition Cathedral in Tula.

Father George Kossov of
Chekriakov Village.

kitchen at the guest house, one morning a monk walked in, of medium height, with large, dark eyes and smiling, exclaimed:

"Oh! A new one! What is your holy name? What province are you from?" And upon hearing that I was Michael and a Tulan, he even more joyfully proclaimed:

"Well, and I was also Misha, but now I am Misail. You have a good name, and you're my fellow countryman. Well, may God grant, may He grant that you will be a monk with us!" He was a hierodeacon and a hieromonk there. In 1914, he was sent to war as a chaplain. After the revolution he served as a hegumen in the palace, where he was arrested and sentenced to be shot. They did not kill him then, but let him go, ordering him sternly: "Do not step foot into a monastery!" He wrote me that he reached the Kaluga region through the woods, over the fields, feeding upon raw mushrooms, berries and bark from the trees. He wrote: "It's horrible what I have endured!" From "Tsarskoe Selo" he walked to the Kaluga province, where he lived in the bath-house of one kind peasant. But after the appearance of articles in the newspapers by Bishop Innocent Pustynsky* directed against monks—saying that they, the monks, have dispersed across Russia like cock-roaches and tell simple folk that the Soviet government is antichrist's and that Christians should not submit to it—the Reds who read it drove all of the monks away to the cold regions where they perished by the thousands. There too perished Fr. Hegumen Misail Zaitsev, the New Priest-martyr.

[1966]

3. New Martyr Father Ioasaph

Now I often, very often, remember the prophetic words of my elder Fr. Ioasaph. My spiritual teacher-elder was the extremely kind monk

---

*Originally he was in America and, because a renovationist, was full of Western reform ideas. After the Revolution, he caused thousands to be persecuted in Russia.

Father Ioasaph Nekrasov, a monk of holy life and education. He often said to me: "Misha, when sorrows, slanders and persecutions come— rejoice in them, venerate them, for this way is the royal path that leads to God." The Elder said much, and all of it has come and is coming to pass for me. Glory be to God for all things.

Already in those distant times, everything was beginning to fall apart in Russia. Of course, even our monasteries did not escape it, and within their massive walls Christian love and brotherhood also languished. The monks were almost all peasants, and everyone knows what kind of life our rural farmer-peasants lived. But even these complained, living in the monastery.

Elder Ioasaph often said to me during those years: "Misha, do you hear how the monks complain? The food is bad, and this and that! Misha, complaining is a terrible sin. For murmuring God's chosen people, the Jews, were punished not a few times. Palestine is not far from Egypt, but the Lord led the Jews an entire forty years, and not many of them actually reached the promised land. Do you see what a terrible sin it is—murmuring against God? And what do the monks have to complain about? They have both warm cells and good food, they can eat bread to their hearts content! They have both shoes and clothing. But the peasant has a family and inadequacies, harvest failure and head-taxes to pay. After all, they bear many hard times without complaint. Ach, Misha, God will send us terrible trials, will take everything away from us, and then can we say: 'It is bad for us; we have nothing to eat.' Misha, this will come to pass if we do not repent. God will spare neither our rich churches, nor belltowers, nor bells, nor all our brotherhood. Everything, everything will be taken away because of our sinful complaining.

The Elder spoke so sorrowfully, with pure tears in his eyes. [He himself was starved to death in 1918 and died a martyr's death.]

I will add that the disaster that befell Russia, the persecutions of Christ's Church and of monasteries, was foreseen by other monks and holy hierarchs, and by priests and pious lay people.   [1963]

* * *

Oh, how I loved to watch the marvelous tonsure ceremony—"the monastic wedding." Yes, truly at that moment, when they stood at the ambo so joyfully, happily—earthly angels, the grace of God shone in their faces, and I recalled the words of St. Seraphim, "Why cannot a man serve God as do the angels?" [1966]

* * *

There were youths from poor families who did not think about monasteries. In our town of Alexin, my comrades said to me: "Misha, where are you off to? A monastery is a grave, but you are young, happy, love flowers, music, and here you are leaving for the stone walls of a monastery." [1959]

5. Two Elders Named Gerasim

I knew one elder-ascetic, the founder of the St. Sergius Monastery in Kaluga diocese, Fr. Hegumen Gerasim. His elder, Hieromonk Gerasim (†1896) was of holy life and clairvoyant (founder of the Iveron Monastery). His disciple, Fr. Hegumen Gerasim (†1918) served in such a way that he forced one to pray. His successor, Fr. Hegumen Avkensentius, an educated man and first-class singer (he attended the synodal school of music in Moscow) wrote to Fr. Archimandrite Simeon in New York about the death of Elder Gerasim. He died in July [31st] of 1918. It was terribly hot. In the upper church were large windows, and it was very difficult to pray on hot days as it was very stuffy. Elder Gerasim, his mortal body, was there for ten days and there was no decomposition. [Fr. Simeon] a monk of righteous life wrote about it.* He had served until the First World War at the Russian Mission of the Holy City of Jerusalem. He had an excellent bass voice. Bishop Evdokim gave me my name in memory of these two ascetics—

---

*See *Russky Palomnik* no. 16, 1997. pp. 132-134, and Appendix II below.

Elder Gerasim of St. Tikhon's.   Elder Gerasim the Younger.

St. Tikhon's Monastery.

Gerasims. They were both Michaels in the world, and Gerasims of the Jordan. Now I do not know what became of those places.   [1964]

* * *

In St. Tikhon's Monastery labored Hieromonk Gerasim [I], the founder of the Iveron Mother of God Convent. I remember also that Convent and his grave there. He was buried in the underground church, and over his grave was built a metal case which was very artistically made. On it hung his heavy, iron chains. Everything that decorated the dear, cozy church had been donated by a pious merchant, a venerator of Fr. Gerasim. I knew his two disciples: Fr. Hegumen Gerasim, the founder of the St. Sergius Monastery, which was located six versts from the St. Tikhon Monastery, and Hieromonk Fr. Jeremiah. They were all tonsured in St. Tikhon's Monastery.   [1962]

* * *

I began to think about monasticism at the age of eight, and I came to love this path. I joined the monastery on the 17th of July, 1906, old style. In that same year was the young Hieromonk Alexei Simansky appointed as the rector of the seminary in Tula, who later became the Patriarch. I met him in the office of Bishop in 1915, in the Alexander Nevsky Lavra.

Everything in Russia was so quiet, calm, and people rejoiced and loved life. There was plenty of everything, and it was all cheap. I visited many places and saw a great deal. Everywhere life flowed peacefully, calmly, and our peasants did not think about revolution or the removal of the Tsar. I loved to visit our Russian settlements and villages, where life flowed peacefully. Our peasants did not live richly, but they had all they needed. Only the drunkards knew calamity. Yes, they were kind folk, who loved to treat guests to all they had. Our artist Korovin wrote much about this.

All over Russia during the summer you could hear the singing of Russian songs, and it was often so wonderful, so sad, as only our simple Russian folk can sing. Living in the holy monastery, working in the infirmary, I opened the window to my cell and listened lovingly to the beautiful Russian songs. And they had such remarkable, strong voices, that even from far away I understood all of the words of their folk songs. I love my dear homeland and Russian nature.

Sometimes I dream that I am in Russia, that my cell stands in the meadow, surrounded by birches, and the bright sun shines from the sky. Lord, I think to myself—now I am home, in Russia, in my native land and how happy am I! But when I wake up, I see that I am in Alaska far from my native land—and my heart begins to wail painfully.   [1946]

6. New Martyr Jonah

The abbot of the St. Tikhon Monastery, Fr. Hegumen Jonah, wrote to me: "My dear, living far away from our holy monastery, you cry over it. But I live next to it, see its churches, its bell tower, its wall, and at times I sit and sing: 'Adam sits across from paradise'—and tears flow." But now Fr. Jonah is in the Heavenly Monastery, after enduring those terrible years. He was a good monk, served and read beautifully. I left that place in August, 1911. There was wonderful nature there, a magnificent pine forest on sandy ground, oak trees, birch trees, lindens, and an alder grove. Heaven upon the earth.   [1959]

✳ ✳ ✳

Oh, how I loved it, when I would step inside the Cathedral in the Monastery of St. Tikhon, and lampadas flickered in the dim light. Near St. Tikhon's coffin, around his reliquary, there were fifty-three lampadas. Several of them were massive, silver-leafed. How beautiful it was when they were all lighted. I have loved the lampada from my childhood.

> Before an old icon a lamp-light is flickering,
> Throwing a shadow on a ceiling so low,
> Thought after thought, bitter thoughts bickering,
> Now with each other of times long ago.

ABBA GERASIM AND HIS LETTERS

How I remember her standing so tenderly,
Clasping her hands, barely hiding her fears
Over my sick bed, she prayed so motherly
The icon-light trembling in each of her tears.

A Poem by Nikitin   [1959]

* * *

During the Dormition fast I remember my Monastery of St. Tikhon, its beautiful cathedrals—that of the Transfiguration and that of the Holy Dormition. Wonderful services, thousands of pilgrims. And what ringing of bells! There were talented bell-ringers, who induced one to listen to the wondrous music. The large bell weighed 1,000 poods, and the second-largest 600 poods. It was wonderful how they rang the treble peal. All our Russia had a wealth of bells. But now they are silent.

The Tula Monastery (Shchelgov) was located about three versts from the city of Tula and was surrounded by beautiful birch groves. There were no huge bells in its belfry, but the ones it did have were made to order by a millionaire, and of course the collection was lavish. Monk Dionysius was an artist in his own right; he would ring out church music on the bells. Happy Tula merchants would come there in the summertime to pray and stroll in the pure air, and also to listen to the marvelous music of the bells. When they treated Fr. Dionysius heartily, he would treble-ring and play so well on the bells, that the happy merchants would cry. He rang out wonderfully melancholy: "With the saints give rest...." Why did all that was wonderful and beautiful disappear? Well, now I am falling apart, I want to cry. Tomorrow I have to serve the Liturgy. It is quiet now. There is no wind. The squall blew over quickly, the trees began to roar. The moon shines in the sky.   [1959]

7. Traditions in the St. Tikhon's Monastery

I lived for more than five years in a large monastery (St. Tikhon's Monastery), where there were over 200 monks, and in my obedience as cell attendant to Archimandrite Lawrence I visited every cell in that monastery. Religious people came to the monastery, and in the holy corner of every monk's cell hung icons, lampadas burning in front of them. Beneath the icons was a corner cabinet where the monk kept his holy book, lamp oil and candles. Every monk from the time he was a novice loved and venerated the Mother of God, and some had excellent icons of Her image. I visited many monasteries, sketes and lavras. I also visited Mt. Athos; its Russian and Greek monasteries. Russian monasteries had many people as well as sketes. Nowhere in our monasteries did they serve meat. True, in some they offered a small glass of wine and some serving of fish. But everything of that sort was preserved in cupboards.   [1963]

✳ ✳ ✳

During Great Lent in 1907 the enormous Transfiguration Cathedral in the Monastery of St. Tikhon was packed with people. The Great Canon of St. Andrew of Crete was read. The weather was damp, and there was still much snow. Water dripped along the walls of the church, and it was very stuffy. They held a long monastic service, and the singing was beautiful, moving. Unforgettable times.

The Dormition Cathedral in town was filled to overflowing with people. Bonfires of candles burned before the locally venerated holy icon; there was moving singing by a full choir: "Have mercy on me, O God, have mercy on me." The canon was read by Batiushka Fr. Nicholas Glagolev, who was loved by all, and he read in such a way that every word penetrated into the soul. Oh, how beautiful are our Orthodox services! And in the monastery, monks in two cliroses called to the Lord with contrition. True, Fr. Archimandrite Lawrence did not read the canon very well. I read it also during the Apostles' fast. In Russia before the revolution people who did not observe the first week of the fast came to hear it and pray. Yesterday after serving the Liturgy of the holy Apostle James I was joyful all day.... Now it is quiet and overcast. But the birds are singing, and they will sing until 10:00 at night.

[June 19, 1961]

* * *

Today I served the Liturgy of the holy Apostle James, the brother of the Lord. The morning was cool, but it was quiet. I love it when the sun's rays permeate the church. After Liturgy I served a moleben. A lovely day. The sun is shining, the sky is blue. My mother's nameday.

Of course I was in a blessed state of soul—I know that my dear mother also prays for me from the other world. When I lived in Kaluga province, I came every year to Alexin for this day. Oh, what joy there was! I arrived in town late in the evening. As I remember, each time the weather was lovely, warm. In our parlor the windows would be open, the gardenias, asters and petunias would still be in bloom. A million crickets chirped. The first night we did not even sleep, mama and I.... Where have you flown, you lovely, happy days?

Our quiet town of Alexin, spread across the high bank of the river Oka, is surrounded by woods and various sorts of trees. To the south flows the Oka, and the view from the cathedral hill is very picturesque, especially on moonlit evenings and nights. On the west and north side grows a lush pine grove, where there were many beautiful summer houses. How beautiful it was there during spring and summer! In the distance, three to four versts away, there grew birch and oak trees, and pretty meadows, scattered with wildflowers. I was always amazed at how in those emerald grasses there were never any weeds. Some meadows were round, some square or oblong, but it was just as if someone had planted the trees around their edges.

г. Алексинъ. Вокзалъ.

Alexin railroad station. Pre-revolutionary postcard.

General view of the city of Alexin, on the Oka River.

There were also such meadows not far from the monastery, where we young novices went on feast days to play a game of lapta. How simple it all was, good and happy. Of course, at 4:00 we hurried to the monastery to have tea and go to vespers. In the summer the gate closed at 9:00, and we were able to walk along the shadowy road and admire the fireflies. Oh, how wonderful it was! Now that old age creeps up and the bones ache, you think, was it all a dream?

[August 26/September 8, 1950]

* * *

In Russia, all monks went to church in their mantles. They wore it over their podrazniks. During the first week of Great Lent, all wore what was given to them at tonsure. But I loved to see monks in the church in the mantle and klobuk.... Matins were at 2:00 in the morning. How good it was to come early, early to God's church, where the lampadas quietly flickered, at times candles, where there was quiet, melancholy singing, where monks stood like deathly shadows by the walls of the magnificent cathedral....   [1942]

* * *

It is hard to kill people's souls. They wrote to me from the Kaluga region, the place where there used to be a spring of St. Tikhon and where there were wooden buildings. The Bolsheviks destroyed everything and burned them down. But the water which bubbles out for ages is impossible to destroy. A hieromonk Job wrote to me, having visited our native places after twenty-five years. He was in Siberia and wrote: "On the place there was a church and bathhouse. Everything was destroyed. But the believing people cut spruce branches and created a form of wall between the men's and women's bathing place, and where they submerged themselves into the holy spring. There also in St. Tikhon's Monastery are resting in the graves friends of Elder Herman—Schemamonk Sergius and Hieroschemamonk Alexander."* O

---

* Yanovsky; see below.

Семенъ Ивановичъ Яновскiй.
1834—1852.

SIMEON IVANOVICH YANOVSKY,
in monasticism Schemamonk Sergius (1789-1876)

my dear St. Tikhon's Monastery, how beautiful you were before the thrice-cursed revolution. Now I am old and weak and how I wish to lay my bones in my dear hermitage. Bishop Ambrose did not deign to visit Ouzinkie nor Spruce Island. They don't need me. I am not theirs. I belong to *Carlovatski*. People have become evil now.   [1965]

* * *

I left St. Tikhon's Monastery at the end of August, 1911 and I entered that monastery on the 17th of July in 1906. When I remember all that, my heart begins to moan, and a tear falls from my eyes. And now antichrist is walking all over Russia with his servants and is destroying the temples of God. And already many of our ancient holy places have been destroyed, whose very stone walls wafted the fragrance of incense. I remember my pious aunt, how she used to say: "O God, prevent us living in those days when in the Russian land they will begin to demolish temples!!" She would rarely leave her room, where she had a multitude of icons and where many icon lamps were perpetually burning.   [1942]

8. ATHONITE IMPRESSIONS

All of my life I dreamed of secluding myself on Mt. Athos, in the desert. On the Feast of the Protection in 1911, I left Russia and went to Mt. Athos over the stormy Black Sea. I remember the monastery feast day in the Monastery of Great Martyr Panteleimon. Athos, my precious Athos!!! On my nameday, the Feast of St. Michael (I was still Michael, 23 years old), November 8/21, we drank tea during talks [at St. Andrew's Skete]. I was young there, and at that time it was too early for me to begin such a life [of a desert dweller]. In St. Andrew's Skete there were churches built on top of the living quarters. On tall buildings there were roofs which were spread with cement, and on the platform a church was built. Oh, how beautifully it was all built there. In the

St. Andrew's Athonite Russian skete, as it looks today.

St. Elias Skete, founded by St. Paisius Velichkovsky.

summer one could pray outside the church and hear everything. Standing on the platform one saw only the sky, the sea and islands in the distance. This was on the east side. To the southeast shone the spire of Athos, its white cliffs.   [1950]

* * *

Russian monasteries on Mt. Athos—St. Andrew's, St. Elias Skete, New Thebaid—all adorned the mountain of Athos. There were more of them on the northeast side, where are more sloping areas, more trees and bush. On their churches were Russian cupolas, painted blue and shining with gold crosses. And the ringing carried far from the Russian bell towers. Very often, sitting on the balcony on the fifth floor, which was on the eastern side, I admired the remarkable nature of Athos, and sang: "And how lovely the panorama of sea, when the sun's ray does burn away." Yes, it was very beautiful!!! Sometimes the ringing of my own, dear Russian belltowers would reach me....

In St. Andrew's Skete in 1911-12, there were over 500 monks (in St. Panteleimon's were over 2,000 including metochia, in St. Elias' 350), a magnificent cathedral and sixteen churches. But dearest to me was the church of St. Innocent, bright and beautiful with five domes. Very beautiful and just as grand was the Church of the Mother of God. It was not a skete, but a magnificent lavra. I lived eight months in that Skete. But, oh my God, how wonderful it was on Mt. Athos in 1912 on the Paschal night. That holy Pascha is hard to forget.... On Good Friday, Hieromonk Seraphim was canonarch, and he read splendidly. I can even picture him, hear his voice. Oh, what a marvelous service on Good Friday. Pascha was on March 25 and the roses were already in bloom, lilies white as snow.... I dreamt of visiting again on my way back from America. At the end of 1911 I read a rough draft of a translation of the prophecy of Elder Nilus about the fate of Athos....*

---

* *The Posthumous Discourses of St. Nilus*, Moscow, 1912.

Now, on Athos Fr. Nikon passed away, as well as his brother Vasily Nicholaevich Shtraumn in Washington. Fr. Nikon stayed with me on Afognak for a month. He lived in Karoulia [on the southern side of Athos, where the most severe hermits lived].

New Thebaid is picturesquely flung across the Western hills. In 1911 there were hundreds of little stone buildings, buried in the foliage of cypress, pine, olive, and grape vines and various bushes. The hut-cells were white with red roofs. Other huts were built upon tall cliffs.... I do not know if Krumitsa still exists on the edge of Athos.

Many of my friends that I knew on Mt. Athos left Athos even before the Second World War. There was some sort of diabolic temptation— the confusion created by the "Name of God" heresy. Those who left the Holy Mountain were then unable to return, although they repented of their error. That was decreed by the ecumenical patriarch. I know that many were very sorry that they had left Mt. Athos. Many of them were good, kind monks. But also with them was the highly educated hieromonk and former officer Anthony Bulatovich. He knew several languages. [1961]

* * *

My father's aunt was wealthy and religious; she sent aid to the monks of Mt. Athos. They, of course, sent her holy icons and books, which I read. My father died at age 52. He caught a cold and was sick for three years. My poor mother died at age 62 from famine somewhere in the village, alone. Typhus was then raging in Russia. Because of the famine, everyone was scattering around Russia. But several people did come to her funeral. The old ladies told my sister Anna that during her last days she often remembered her son who was in America. We were not rich, but mother observed all the fasts, and fasted on Wednesdays and Fridays. Not only we, but also millions of Russian people. And when we fasted, we did not even use oil. [1950]

*** *** ***

My father's parents died in just the same manner as Ivan C. Shmelev describes his father's death, about which I am not able to read without tears. I did not witness the death of my mother, nor of my father. Papa, Alexander Georgivich, died on April 17/30, 1912, and I was on Mt. Athos at that time. Mother, Natalia Ivanovna, died March 4, 1920. She died somewhere in the village of Senino.

I remember, when they boiled incense in the Skete of St. Andrew during Great Lent, the fragrance carried throughout the corridors. They poured the mixture onto marble slabs. In 1911, in November in the Skete of St. Andrew on Mt. Athos I had a dream, that I was as if in Kiev, at the tomb of holy Great Martyr Barbara, whom I venerate and to whom I pray that she might save me from sudden death. I dreamt that I was on my knees at her tomb, praying to her. I arose to venerate and saw that she lay there alive. In Kiev her relics had no head, and in its place lies an icon, showing the head of the holy Great Martyr Barbara. Seeing her alive I became frightened, again fell to my knees, and began to implore her. I said to her: "I read how you suffered for Christ." She answered me quietly, meekly: "It is impossible to describe all that I have suffered." Then I began to beg her: "Take me to where you are? It is hard to live on earth." She answered, "No, it is not time yet for you to die; you will live a long time." Since that night fifty years have passed, difficult years. In the course of these years I have been three times engulfed by the sea and have been sick many times. In 1935 at the end of December, when I fell into the sea and swam in my clothes, I suddenly though: "No, I will not die yet. Holy Great Martyr Barbara will save me; I always pray to her." After that I do not remember anything. But the cold water, which took a lot out of me, did not damage my lungs. It is true that I caught a cold, but I did not take any medicine, I prayed instead.

The bolsheviks are responsible for the demise of Russian monasticism on Mt. Athos. In Petrograd there was an excellent Athos Metochion. At first the Bolsheviks expelled the monks and forbade them to live

An old Kaluga photograph of monks who were friends of Fr. Gerasim.
At the back right is his close friend John-Barsanuphius,
who died as Schemamonk Basil on Mt. Athos.

Alexei Pushkarev, a friend of
Ryassaphore-monk Gerasim,
a student of the Tula
Classical Gymnasium

Fr. Barsanuphius, friend of Fr. Gerasim.
Picture sent from Mt. Athos.

in the city. But could it have been easy for them to travel from far away to serve in the church? They submitted a request to the Greek consulate for visas to leave for Athos. But for that they were all arrested and sent north, where they all perished.   [1958]

* * *

All of the faithful in Russia venerated Mt. Athos, hearing that ascetics lived there. So one decides to go to the Holy Mountain to pray and breathe in the sanctity. He arrives and is met there on the Holy Mountain by a derelict, tattered (and dishevelled) man in an old riassa and Athonite hat. This is a "siromach," and what does he (the pilgrim?) know about "siromach"? They live on their own, rent rooms for pennies and beg in wealthy monasteries. They are under no authority. It is true that amongst them are some real doers of prayer; but those rarely leave their cells, and then usually in order to receive the Divine Mysteries in a nearby monastery. Good, kind, God-fearing monks. But it is true that some of them dishonor Athonite monasticism by their behavior. 1911 was the year of my visit on the wondrous Holy Mountain. How I would have liked to have been there during holy and Great Lent.... Wonderful cathedrals, paraclyses there are beautiful.... I had the chance to venerate the Iveron Mother of God Icon on Mt. Athos.

9. AFOGNAK IN ALASKA

Today I served a pannikhida for Bishop Nestor and the Athonite Hieromonk Nestor, who was the Abbot of the Annunciation Monastery after Elder Fr. Hieroschemamonk Parthenius. Bishop Nestor of Alaska was a very kind person. In 1916, when I arrived in Alaska, many of the old ones who knew and loved Bishop Nestor were still among the living. He was one of the German Barons Von Saas, and not Von Sakis, about whom Metropolitan Theophil wrote. Could you find such a holy hierarch in our time?   [November 10, 1961]

Kodiak Harbor, 1910, as it looked when Fr. Gerasim arrived there.

Sitka Cathedral synaxis, headed by Bishop Philip in the middle, and Fr. Gerasim, last cleric on the right front. 1916.

✳ ✳ ✳

In 1916 I came to Alaska, to Sitka, together with Bishop Philip and Deacon Anthony. And since then I am ending up my lifelong pastoral path at the grave of Righteous Elder Herman. Much I had here to endure for these long years and pain and human injustice. Much changes I saw: Some archpastors and pastors came and soon went away but I have grown to feel myself as a native and I love this poor, harsh nature, cold fogs, the sea storms—winds, spruce forest and it seems to me that I will also find my eternal rest in the vicinity of my dear grave of Elder Herman.

Today passed exactly forty-two years since my arrival on Kodiak Island. That year [1917] the winter was very severe and very stormy, from Sitka I travelled on a post schooner that was dirty and smelly. It took us only five days to reach Juneau. In Juneau I transferred to a larger ship, "Admiral Evens." All the way to Kodiak our traveling was very stormy. In one strait we were surrounded by huge mounds of ice, and the steamer went more calmly. I will not hide that I was afraid and was praying. O how frightening was the terrible sea.

From Juneau to Kodiak it took ten days. And everywhere that the steamer stopped I saw mounds of snow.

In those days, forty-two years ago, Kodiak appeared as a Russian village. It looked pitiful and poor to me. All the little houses were packed with mountains of snow. It was hard to walk on the little path and the western wind was cold and harsh.

Oh, how I grieved arriving in Kodiak alone and in such time of the year! I will not hide even this, that at night, in the church house, I bitterly, bitterly wept.

Those days Kodiak was adorned with our Orthodox Church surrounded with trees. And entering its walls, I at once felt that I arrived on my native land, somewhere in Holy Russia!

Everything there was Russian, beautiful and my own! Icons were of beautiful artistry and old craftsmanship. As for church utensils, they were such that even in Russia some cities didn't have them.

Young, carefree Fr. Gerasim, as "bishop" of brooms.

Of course, as I walked under the vaults of this Church, I involuntarily remembered the antiquity of my own dear Church at home, and those times when there lived Russian monks and Russian people and there was waving in the air a three-colored flag.

Of course then I remembered also Elder Father Herman whose things then were treasured in Kodiak: that poor kamilavka, chains and copper cross.

Then I was sad and rejoiced at the same time that I came to such a place where the Word of God was preached by our first enlighteners, Russian Orthodox monks. That was in 1917 and how everything has changed now here. Kodiak now has turned into a town, there are new big and small houses. The church there is also new. And there appeared different kinds of preachers and different people. From the old beautiful, quiet Kodiak, there remained almost nothing.   [1959]

***

In Alaska I was submerged three times in the cold ocean waters. The last time was near Afognak, in the month of March on a terribly cold day. Some drunken Aleuts were taking me there, and their boat had become disjointed through weathering. We loaded my things onto the boat and headed for the shore. I noticed that the boat was quickly filling with water, so that oarsman steered the boat towards the cape, to the nearest shore; and the boat struck a large and sharp rock. We took the suitcases and submerged ourselves in the cold water. Oh, and here was a hot bath! But we had to—in the suitcases were church articles. It was already dark, and there was a strong, cold westerly wind. I thought that it was the end of me. I caught a chill and had a bad cough, but remained among the living.   [1961]

***

Yes, I have seen everything in these 44 years in Alaska. Now priests fly in airplanes. But we, the paupers, ride in kayaks, open boats with paddles! Or, when the opportunity arises, on stinking schooners. Sometimes we were as long as a month en route. But now it is time for me to get ready to go "home." High time! Soon I will reach the age of 72! But how hard it is to leave my beloved desert hermitage! All of these years here it was clean, cozy. Are there any monks to be found who would live here? Fr. Sergius Irtel wanted to come here ... and Fr. Elias Shchukin [ten years before him], but....   [1960]

10. A Paschal Visit to St. Herman's Grave

Finally, the Lord made me worthy to spend time on Spruce Island, called "New Valaam" and, after my ten-year stay in Alaska, to visit the grave of the wondrous Elder-missionary, Monk Herman.

May 14/27, on a quiet, sunny morning, we set out from Kodiak with Fr. Protopriest Nicholas Kashevarov and two godly women-pilgrims in an open boat for Spruce Island and the Elder's grave. In an hour and a half we had already arrived at the shore of "New Valaam." With a feeling of great joy I stepped upon the shores of the island, where the great ascetic laborer lived for nearly half a century, the man of fiery prayer, with a crystal-pure soul, the first Orthodox missionary in this—at one time—wild, pagan country: Fr. Herman.

Along the narrow path we began to ascend into the thicket of forest to the Elder's place of eternal rest, to his grave. The area is hilly. The spruce forest is a thick forest. Quiet, sunny weather. Tall, 100-year-old spruce trees, the only witnesses of the Elder's solitary ascetic labors. The singing of the feathered dwellers of the desert involuntarily bore one away to thoughts of those bygone years when Elder Herman lived here. And so it seemed that at any moment the figure of the Elder might appear from the thicket—his meek face—and he would give us a word of consolation. One is reminded, by the similitude of surroundings and of the very faces, of another wondrous Elder, St. Seraphim of Sarov. He was actually Fr. Herman's contemporary! The latter greatly venerated the Sarov Elder and had his portrait in his cell.

We entered the meadow, which was surrounded by tall spruce trees. On this occasion it was bathed in the rays of the spring sun. In the meadow we saw a white, wooden monument on the site of the Elder's blessed repose. We all went down on our knees and prayed there, where for more than forty years Fr. Herman prayed ardently to God the Lord, prayed ardently and fervently. Here he conducted spiritual warfare with the enemy of mankind—the devil—and here he was made worthy, undoubtedly, to see wondrous visions with his spiritual eyes. Here at this site he shone, like a bright candle, through his equal-to-the-apostles service to God and man. Here, to his poor cell, came during his lifetime all the humiliated and offended; and the Elder received all, consoling them and praying for them. Here at this place he fed from his own hands bears and ermine. Here he labored in the sweat of his brow, carrying seaweed from the seashore for fertilizer, with which he planted various vegetables. There were rows of his garden which were still marked, even though ninety years have passed since the day of his repose. Here did the righteous one fall asleep in the eighty-first year of his much-laboring life, leaning over the book "The Acts of the Apostles," on December 13, 1837. [Actually on November 15, 1936.]

Having prayed at the monument, we began to climb higher up the hill to the Elder's gave. Before we reached the church, we saw a spring with clear water. Even during the Elder's lifetime the sick drank from this spring; and through their deep faith in the Elder's sanctity, many of the sick came to Spruce Island to drink of this water and took it away with them, like a sacred thing, partaking of it during times of sickness.

Having drunk the cold, clear waters of St. Herman's Spring, we went to the church, which is already visible from the spring through the gigantic trees. And here is the church. It is not very large, wooden, skirted with boards, painted white.

We enter the church. There it is, that wonderworking grave of the Elder-laborer, under the vault of the humble church dedicated to the Valaam Sts. Sergius and Herman. On the right side, in the form of a coffin, was a grave-cover built over the Elder's grave, covered with an

Wooden memorial with an icon, erected on the spot where
St. Herman's cell stood. It was almost gone when
Fr. Gerasim first came to the island on May 27, 1927.

ornamental cloth and strewn with flowers. On the wall hangs an icon in large format with a gold, gilt frame of Sts. Sergius and Herman with St. Nicholas. The icon is painted very artistically and looks as though it had just left the artist's brush.

Having vested in the altar, I came out to serve a moleben before the icon of Sts. Sergius and Herman. I served the moleben to Sts. Sergius and Herman and St. Seraphim, whose portrait was located right there in the church, that very portrait that was in Elder Herman's cell during his lifetime. It is remarkable, also, that the portrait of Elder Seraphim was not in the least damaged, even though it is printed on simple paper; it looks as though it is perfectly new.* It is necessary to note that it is always damp in the church. Up until the time the church was built, the portrait was located in a poor earthen hut, which from the time of the Elder's death was never heated. St. Seraphim was portrayed walking to his hermitage in a rough white cassock with an axe in his hand. The Elder's face is the face of an ascetic. I have never seen a portrait of the Elder like this one, and it seems to me that he should have been like this, judging from his great labors and ascetic life. At the moleben I commemorated Metropolitan Platon and all bishops and missionaries working in Christ's fields in America.

After the moleben I served a pannikhida. I commemorated also the names of the reposed hierarchs who labored in the Mission, and the Elder's friends, Valaam monks. How good it was to pray before the grave of the Elder, how light and joyful in soul!

After the pannikhida I lifted the floor boards and went down to the Elder's grave. On the grave lay a wooden cross, which had been placed there on the funeral day of Fr. Herman. Although the cross had lain on the ground in the dampness—and it had been around already for ninety years—it was still strong and had not given over to decomposition, even

---

*This engraving was there in 1961. I saw it on the north wall near the door, but by 1983 when I visited again it was gone. They say it was taken to New York's seminary. Why? Its place is in that chapel until the end of time.—A. H.

though it was made out of spruce, which rots very quickly here. On the cross were small icons carved into the cross-point. I took some earth from the Elder's grave as a remembrance. Having closed up the floor once more, and closing up the church, we again descended to the seashore.

On the way back we returned to the place of the Elder's blessed repose. When I approached the monument, I sensed a fragrance in the air. At first I thought that it was from Fr. Nicholas' clothing, but he was dressed in a coat. The fragrance was so subtle, pleasant.... I fell to my knees again and said: "I thank you, kind Elder Fr. Herman, that you made me worthy to visit with you in this beloved place. Christ is Risen!"

Then I also said: "Fr. Herman, if I come to your little hermitage, accept me; I have come to love this place."

Bidding farewell to this wondrous little corner, we descended to the shore and left for Kodiak upon the quiet waters of the ocean, beneath the caressing rays of the spring sun.   [1935]

11. LIFE ON SPRUCE ISLAND

Tomorrow, [July] 11 (June 29) is the commemoration of the Valaam Wonderworkers Sergius and Herman. Elder Fr. Herman's nameday. I have already prepared everything for services. I awoke early to bake prosphora and litia loaves. The church was swept and cleaned long ago. The soul becomes sad to think about Valaam, what became of it. I never managed to visit it, our Russian northern Athos. Of course, I read a great deal about it, about its ascetic laborers. But I also heard much from the lips of monks, who spiritually labored there. Life there was more severe than on Athos. Mt. Athos was different; there are many independent communities, which ran individually under the direction of their own elders. Much is ruined there by wine and crab, which is freely available there and cheap. But of course there have been glorious spiritual laborers there.... I read again Shmelev's "Pilgrimage" and often shed tears. Everything in it is so close to the heart, so dear. Well, that is enough, or I will start to cry again.

On the spot where Fr. Elias Shchukin lived it is all overgrown with pine. [This is on Icon Bay on Spruce Island.] River beavers have inhabited the lake and furrowed it. The house that was built there was removed to the shore below, near the stream. But it is also falling to ruin without any repairs or painting. All the dollars that were collected to build the monastery have disappeared. Lord forgive them.... In the hermitage I serve alone and expect no one. It is cold now, the stove should have been stoked earlier. Our hierarchs do not know abut my life in Alaska all of these forty-six years! [1963]

***

We fixed the church over Elder Herman's grave. We replaced all of the columns, put in new trimming, new double floors. We also built a new entrance, completely different, with a window; and now it is bright there. Also the walls are put up, and the floors are covered with boards. A staircase was built. We also skirted the lower parts with boards. We managed to paint it once. But, at that, the church could not be better, it has a cheerier look. Now it involuntarily reminds one of a skete—a skete church. Were there three or four monks it would be a skete! And this place would be perfect for a skete. All ascetics fled to the woods, to wild islands. Mt. Athos is all like a desert; there are no women there. But lay people live there; there is a town and trade. But some monks, lovers of the desert life, the solitary life, settled on such craggy places that it is terrifying even to climb. They love their places, their poor cells, and do not grow tired of living there. To him who has God in his heart, who keeps Him always in remembrance, the desert seems to be paradise! Our hierarchs, who wrote about the Spruce Island Hermitage, did not think at all about such a skete. No, they thought of a missionary community, as the Catholics have. [1945]

Painting of St. Herman by Fr. Gerasim's friend,
Archimandrite Seraphim Oblivantsev, 1935.

* * *

Fr. Herman's nameday is June 28, old style, the commemoration day of the Valaam Wonderworkers…. Yes, I believe that the saints pray for those who love them and venerate them. I do not remember where or which righteous woman it was who was buried in a monastery and for whom the monks for many years burned lampadas near her grave, but after several years they abandoned the practice; and that righteous one appeared to the father abbot in a dream, and said: "I am with the Lord in heaven and in blessedness. When you burned the lampada at my grave, your love for me made me pray more fervently for you at the throne of God." I love the glow of that little holy flame; and I, wherever I may have lived, always burned lampadas—just as did my marvelous Aunt Alexandra Georgievna, in monasticism Angelina.   [1962]

* * *

After the earthquake I happened to come to the hermitage on July 11/24, and served on the 15th/28th and 16th/29th, on the commemoration of St. Tikhon of Kaluga. I decorated the small chapel with alder brances, and the colored lampadas and candles flickered. Of course, I remembered the unforgettable Monastery of St. Tikhon, the brothers, and prayed for them. But it was sad to sing the stichera to the saint, in which St. Tikhon's Monastery is mentioned. I remembered that entire marvelous scene, of the monastery before the revoltuion.

Our chapels [after the tidal wave] were unharmed; only the candles fell. In the small chapel, the lampadas did not even shatter. Neither did the glass case over the Elder's poor kamilavka. Bishop Ambrose, after March 27, visited Kodiak and served, but he did not write anything to me. Only later did he write from Sitka, but not about Spruce Island or about the holy relics—not a word!   [1964]

* * *

On May 14/27, 1926, I visited Spruce Island for the first time—that marvelous place; and there, near the wooden monument where now

Fr. Gerasim sits on the beach of Monks' Lagoon with his dog Brownie.

stands a chapel, when I fell to my knees and said, "Fr. Herman, Christ is Risen!", I was surrounded by a heavenly fragrance. This I said: "Fr. Herman, if I come to your hermitage, receive me; I have come to love this place." [1961]

* * *

In 1935 I came to Spruce Island, to Elder Herman's Hermitage. The sun penetrated my cell between the logs where there is a fissure through which I can see the dog Brownie [outside]. I had to patch up and fill up the holes. I could not buy anything: I had only fifty dollars, and winter that year was very cold. At the end of December I went to Ouzinkie, where I served in the church and worked in Mr. Grimes' store. I needed to pay a debt. There I received an order for embroidery and I earned a little and built a chapel near my cell, on the spot where Fr. Herman's cell was. In the spring of 1936, the famous Archimandrite Theodosius Kulchitsky, a friend of Metropolitan Leonty, came and exploded in front of the people: "It was entirely unnecessary to build a chapel here. What kind of holiness is here? He only ate and slept here." His words offended even my Aleuts; they murmured against him. But I was glad that the Lord helped me to build it. Now I have served in it twenty-two years. Of course, I served also in the church—the Vladimir Icon of the Mother of God is there. It is old and well painted. Yes, I preserve that holy object here in hopeful cleanliness. I have everywhere tidied and ornamented God's church. I often think about it: will there be anyone after me to take my place? [1950]

* * *

I dug a grave for my dog Brownie, lined it with moss, wrapped Brownie in a sheet and buried him. I cried, bitterly cried. It sometimes happens that from great sorrows, from a longing for his homeland, a man becomes nervously ill and does not know what to do.

On Spruce Island I have MY OWN cell and MY OWN chapel. The large chapel I cleaned up completely—icons, lampadas and carpets. The interior is all my doing. It is not true what they wrote in the *American*

Orthodox Messenger, that I asked someone to set me up on Spruce Island. This is their new lie. I have my own cell, my own chapel. This is in accordance with the rules of Mt. Athos. [1952]

❋ ❋ ❋

It has been written, more than once, that Fr. Herman's prophecy has been fulfilled, that a monk like himself, fleeing the glory of men, will come and live on Spruce Island in his chosen hermitage. But I have never ascribed such a thing to myself. Yes, I love my quiet hermitage and leave it with bitter tears, rejoicing when I return to it; and solemnly, with tender feeling, I kiss the holiness there. All of these years I have never tired of being there, although I do not see people for weeks, even months. I was never sad even during the winter months, there in the snow-covered hermitage. Yes, it is clear that the love of Christ is dying in the souls of modern hierarchs, priests and monks. The hierarchs, Amphilocus, Alexis and John, have tried to expel me from Spruce Island: squeezed, slandered and contrived various things against me. [1964]

❋ ❋ ❋

They painted the small chapel for me white with brown trim. Were there money, I would build a new, more solid one. My heart aches when I think: what will happen to this place when I die? All these years, twenty-seven years, I rested in soul there. Elder Herman received me so affectionately. I never received anything from the states, where there are so many wealthy parishes. But I always burn a lamp there. I hear that correspondence with me has been forbidden, since I sent three or four copies of the letters sent to me from Archbishop Alexander Nemilovsky. [1962]

❋ ❋ ❋

Being alone and without means, I could not build anything on Spruce Island. And no one desires to live in the desert. Our Russian hieromonks did not want to come here; they love the parish life. Will those who are now tonsured in America ever really go to Alaska? [1962]

12. Vladimir Icon of the Theotokos

Not long ago I received for the Spruce Island Church a precious gift: an ancient icon of the Vladimir Mother of God. It is twelve by ten inches. It has a massive silver frame, old and skillfully made. When and by whom it was painted is unknown. But on the reverse side is written that such and such a lady was blessed with this icon already in 1717. After that, another was blessed with it, Tatiana Alexandrovna, on her birthday, January 3, 1795. E. Petelin's daughter, Lidia of San Francisco, California, bought the icon and gave it to her father, who donated it to the Spruce Island Church. Having received this holy icon, I cleaned off the soot and dust, and cleaned the riza, which then shone brightly like new. Of course, I am glad to have such a gift, but I thought: where were you in Russia, who was your owner, how did you come to America? I believe that this holy icon saw many Russian sorrows and tears of fervently praying Orthodox people. I went to sleep on the night of the eve of January 22, and thought: "How I would like to find a lampada for it!"

On the morning of the 23rd they brought me my mail and your package. I opened it and there was a wonderful, lovely thing about which I had dreamt yesterday: an artistically made lampada. What a joy it was for me! I immediately gave it over to the Mother of God.... All of this is for Elder Herman. [1952]

* * *

During the night and morning it rained. I awoke early, and it was still dark. I began the Liturgy early. I have loved this from my child-hood. After Liturgy, after 10:00, the sky was cleared of its dark clouds and the sun began to shine. When the rain sprinkles the pine needles and the sun comes out, its rays highlighting the trees, the raindrops on the needles play with all the colors of the rainbow—as though everything were scattered with diamonds. How beautiful is God's nature!

[September, 1950]

* * *

The summer was dry, sunny, and the streams all dried up. I walked for water to a stream very far away. I am not in bad health, but my legs grow weak. I carry a container with water and think: St. Tikhon of Kaluga also carried water from far away when he lived alone in the woods. Now I too carry it from far away and pray to my dear abbot, [Tikhon] also to Elder Herman.

[1963]

* * *

In the large chapel is a good icon of St. Tikhon of Zadonsk. I think that it was a gift for Protopriest Tikhon Shalamov.

[1965]

* * *

The Dormition. No one is here today. The birds do not even sing; they all became silent July 31. At 2:00 in the afternoon I went down to the beach where I caught an enormous fish. I brought it home—I am rich! I also found three birch mushrooms [podberezoviki] and several cibarius mushrooms [rizhiki].

[1959]

* * *

It is sad and difficult for an old monk to live in a foreign land. I love my quiet hermitage very much.... I recall my native monastery, God's church, a warm cell. Lord, how good it was in Holy Russia, especially in our sketes, in the shady forests, in birch groves. Oh, birch tree, how I would love to press you to my breast and breathe into my lungs your aroma! There are no birch trees on our island. Everything here is different—it is spruce that covers the entire Spruce Island.

[1958]

13. Desert Woes

Let them talk, revile and slander. Yesterday at vigil I read the Kathisma in Russian, and the Psalms were all sad, the holy Prophet David complains about his enemies, his slanderers. I came to these words: "Why do you despond, my soul, why are you troubled? Hope in the Lord; for I will continue to glorify him, my Savior and my God" … and I shed tears; they enlightened my soul, my tortured heart! That night I slept better, more calmly. I arose early. The morning was cold, the sun illumined the treetops. I served the proskemedia unhurriedly and commemorated very many people. I prayed fervently for my brothers Sergius and Gabriel [hieromonks who committed suicide in the last century in Alaska from despondency and abandonment].* How good and peaceful it is to serve Divine Liturgy in the desert! How grateful I am to God, to the Mother of God, Sts. Sergius and Herman, that they put the thought in my mind to move to the desert. I will not hide the fact that the devil assaulted me for it…. How they have poisoned my mood, people tormented me, our "humble" bishops and Alaskan priests. What have they not said about me. They even contrived to say that I have stuffed away four thousand dollars in Afognak. In Kodiak Pelagia Maliutina and the daughter of Fr. Nicholas Kashevarov,

---

*See the letters of M. Z. Vinokouroff in the Alaska State Library, Juneau. Fr. Gabriel enlisted to be a missionary far away in the north. He was placed in the Nome area, in the Russian mission of St. Michael, where he began to miss civilization to the point of having extreme depression. Upon his request to change location, he was refused by Metropolitan Innocent, which drove him to utter despair. The Sitka Hieromonk Sergius had a similar depression; he also lost hope in God and ended his life in Sitka. The sacrifice that missionaries give beyond their human capabilities is rarely talked about, but it could not but be valued by God. Fr. Gerasim, having found out about their deaths, always prayed for their souls in his cell, shedding copious tears. This information was given to him by Vinokouroff.

Juliana Haitment asked: "What do you need money for? We heard that you have $4,000 in the bank." At that time I had never even been in a bank. When I moved to Spruce Island I had only fifty dollars, which E. Petelin had given me as a gift!! Oh, people, people. Ah. God be with them! Even the Lord Christ was slandered. No, I do not think about stockpiling dollars. Glory be to God, I have never been without a piece of bread or a cup of tea. We have not suffered here what they have suffered in Russia during these forty-three years. No, we have not experienced it! In the eighth ikos of the akathist to the Mother of God "Joy of All Who Sorrow," I love the words "All our lives on the earth are painfully filled with sadness from slanders, attacks, reproaches and other many-faceted misfortunes and disasters...." Or, in the seventh Kontakion: "We are pilgrims and strangers in the earth, according to the words of the apostle: 'misfortunes from our enemies, misfortunes from our relations, misfortunes from false brothers, bearing many losses and sorrows....'" This evening I read that one (the seventh Kontakion). Also, the one to St. Seraphim, my beloved, wondrous Elder. St. Ephraim the Syrian I also love.

I think: life would be even harder for us if we did not have our holy intercessors. Oh, how close they are to us, when we run to them with faith and love! What a consolation St. Seraphim left to those who loved him: "When I am no more, come to me at my grave; come when you have time, the more often the better. Everything that you have on your soul, whatever your sorrow, whatever happens to you, come to me at my grave, falling to the ground as if to one alive and tell me; and I will hear you, and your sorrow will pass away. As though I were alive, talk with me, and I will always be alive for you!" Yes, for those who love Batiushka Fr. Seraphim this is a great consolation!!! I believe that in Holy Russia there are many who love and venerate St. Seraphim. I heard that people go secretly to his hermitage and take away with them pine cones and earth.... Today my soul is at peace. I served joyfully, peacefully. The weather is also nice. The visitors were also all friendly and cheerful, and last night a beautiful moon shone over my desert.

Tonight, however, she is covered by clouds. Yes, the days indeed quickly pass by. The morning air is already cold. [August 16/29, 1960]

* * *

Rain. Fog. There was no mail from Kodiak. I sit at home, being sick. My legs are so heavy. I do not know what awaits me. But may God's will be done in all things. I believe that my heavenly friends—St. Seraphim of Sarov, St. Herman of Alaska, and all the rest—will not abandon me.   [1965]

* * *

I love my little hermitage; for me it is the most holy place. But in such years I can no longer stay there during the winters. [He was seventy-six in 1964.]

It was very cold, a terrible westerly wind was as if ready to tear everything apart. The sea was terrifying; the water swirled in spirals.

[January 25, 1952]

14. Fr. Jonah of Odessa

In 1912, in Odessa I was at liturgy in the cathedral church on the commemoration of the holy Equal-to-the-Apostles Mary Magdalene. Bishop Anatoly Kamensky served, the one who consecrated the chapel on Spruce Island (Sts. Sergius and Herman). The Odessa Cathedral was beautiful, magnificent. It was also located in a beautiful area, on a nice square.

I knew and visited in Odessa Priest Jonah Atamansky. He had a remarkable and consoling vision, described in a letter from Odessa to Mt. Athos. From the 1st to the 2nd of January, 1925, our Fr. Jonah, respected long ago by all for his holy life and pastoral activeness, in the all-night vigil service in his church, commemorating at that time St. Seraphim of Sarov, was in a rapture during the singing of the Great Doxology, that is, "Glory to God in the Highest and on earth peace,

Holy Father Jonah Atamansky, a recently canonized saint of Odessa, Ukraine. A parish priest with a family, he was renowned for being a mystical visionary, clairvoyant and a man of deep prayer. He was known as the "St. John of Kronstadt of the South."

good will among men...." First, a great light shone in the altar. The light was first seen by the church steward and several lay people in the congregation. Fr. Jonah dashed into the altar and ... there he froze, became petrified! They sang the Doxology to the end, and then as usual the troparion to the Saint, then the forefeast—once, twice, three times, in expectation of his beginning the Great Ectenia. He was silent. The choir, perplexed and expectant, began and continued with the same troparions. Thus they sang them ten times or more. Fr. Jonah just stood there looking before him, behind the holy table, where the icon of Christ the Savior was. Then his son-in-law came and took him by the arm and said, "Papasha, they've already finished." Fr. Jonah came to himself.

They sat him down in an armchair, brought ammoniac spirits, rubbed his temples, then led him home and put him to bed. On the next day, that is, January 2, the repose day of St. Seraphim (1833), Fr. Jonah served Liturgy, and in the sermon he told the congregation what he had seen. This is his vision:

The holy Apostle John the Theologian and St. Sergius of Radonezh led St. Seraphim of Sarov by the arms. A little further in front of them walked Christ the Savior in light blue, torn clothing. St. Seraphim turned to the Savior and said:

"Who, O Savior, has rent your clothing?"

The Savior answered: "It is the clerics [priests and bishops] who have torn it."

Again, St. Seraphim asked: "You are again going to suffer?"

The Savior answered: "Be at peace."

Behind St. Seraphim walked Simeon the God-Receiver. After the Savior, followed the Most Holy Mother of God with an omophorion on her arms.

St. Seraphim said further:

"He will be in the same glory as I am, who will fulfill all of the canonical rules of the Orthodox Church, as I fulfilled them."

In conclusion, an epilogue: Thus did Christ the Savior comfort St. Seraphim, who takes care of and prays for the Church, for the Tsar, for the Russian land and for the Russian Orthodox people, and in the person of its priest Jonah Atamansky, all the Russian Orthodox people in Russia and scattered abroad.   [1960]

* * *

I also remember a dream, which I saw in the days of my sorrow, when evil-minded bishops, and priests slandered, persecuted me and bitterly insulted me. Emperor Nicholas Alexandrovich said to me then: "I understand you, I myself experienced all that!" And his eyes were sad.
[1963]

* * *

I sleep little, and poorly. So I wake up, take my prayer rope and pray for all the dead; and I commemorate them at the proskemedia. The living sacrifice is brought for the sins of the dead from the beginning of the world. Fr. Roman Shtürmer commemorates only those who belong to the Platonist jurisdiction. No, not I! I commemorate all. We are all children of one Mother Orthodox Church. We are all children of one Mother, Holy Russia. But how sad is this division in the Church.... Now it is happening everywhere.   [1965]

15. Remembering Tula

Leaving for America with Archbishop Evdokim in 1914, I dreamed: "I will live in America for seven to ten years, and when I return to Russia, if I will be alive, I will travel around Russia, visit her monasteries, sketes, ancient churches; and I will write down all that my eyes have seen." I even made a promise to visit Sarov Monastery, to behold the place where our wondrous Elder St. Seraphim labored. But the Lord did not bring it to pass. But that is not my fault; this is how my life has unfolded.

But it pleased God to send difficult trials to our Russia, to the Russian people, and I did not return to my dear homeland. During these years much has perished there. But thank God that I was able to see Russia before the bloody revolution. It is true, for me now it is very painful, so heavy for me to think of it. For I loved it all fervently.

[1963]

✳ ✳ ✳

In 1914, within the walls of the Protection (in Tula) Metochion, the noblewoman Anna Dimitrievna Ivashkova told me about how the blessed Elder Gerasim [I], founder of the Iveron Convent in Kaluga Province foretold to the three sisters—Catherine, Anna and Elizabeth—what would happen to them and to their inherited property in thirty years. Of course he told them not in words, but by actions then incomprehensible to them. But all three sisters understood and wrote down the month, date and time. What do you know—in exactly thirty years, in November, 1905, in the evening, some men broke in and ransacked their property, leaving it to burn. And who was it? Their very own peasants, with whom they, their father and grandfather had lived in friendship and whom they had helped. When they received freedom, their peasants did not want to leave them and everybody cried. They, the Ivashkovs, thought that all the peasants would lay down their souls for them, and therefore they did not request protection from the government, as did many of their neighboring landowners. After this they sold the land and moved to Tula, where they had a nice house. Yet under the new owners they were kicked out of this house. I do not know how or when Elizabeth and Catherine died, but Anna Dimitrievna wrote to me that their servant Anushka, having a kind soul, took into her own room her former mistress.

I helped her a little. There was such poverty there that there was not even tea: they drank dried carrots. And they, all three sisters, were benefactresses to monasteries and churches, to monks and priests. One of the sisters, Elizabeth, led a life of foolishness for Christ, praying on the church steps and dressing in rags. I believe that she took such a *podvig* upon herself by the blessing of Elder Gerasim [I]. It is amazing that she never visited our Protection Metochion, and when Bishop

Evdokim came to visit their home, she did not even appear. As a righteous one, she of course knew what a dangerous path (renovationism) the learned hierarch would take.

She, Elizabeth, died back when our Metochion was still open, and Anna Dimitrievna, who respected Bishop Evdokim, buried her beneath the vaults of the Protection Church. But afterwards, when the bolsheviks closed the metochion and turned the church into a club, Anna Dimitrievna cried bitterly. She wrote to me, "I saw that Katya did not want Liza to be buried under the Protection Church, but she was silent, and did not want to upset me. Now I cannot go there to have a pannikhida served. I can only visit the All-Saints Cemetery and pray there." I wrote to her: "For her soul the prayer is valuable, for she knows and does not blame you for it." A good, kind, religious family.

[November 14, 1963]

* * *

Back in 1914-15, living in Petrograd, I often visited the grave of Righteous Fr. John of Kronstadt and prayed to him as a pleaser of God (as though he were canonized). He helped me in those years, when I was with Archbishop Evdoki and very poor then. Yes, I had to endure insults, humiliation and rudeness from the learned bishop…. Yes, our learned bishops should understand that even the simple man's heart and soul suffers.

Back in 1914, working in the church of the Protection of the Mother of God in Tula, some sort of depression seized my soul, and someone whispered to me: "Soon all of this will no longer exist." Tears, bitter tears, streamed across my face. I shared it with a few monks, but they told me: "This is despondency, which is sinful. You need to pray." But the same thing happened in Petrograd, where I spent the winters of 1914 and 1915. There I often went to the chapel, where the miracle-working icon of the Mother of God "Joy of All Who Sorrow" was located. At that time a good priest served molebens and read the Akathist. I did not much like to go to the Kazan Cathedral. It was enormous, and lacked the coziness of the smaller church….

In 1915, we met Great Friday in Thessalonica, and at 2:00 we were present at the church of holy Great Martyr Dimitry of Thessalonica. There, over the shroud, was built a black velvet canopy. The plank was low; you had to bend down. Around it on the floor was a mountain of roses of all colors. I then felt sorry that they were not in vases with water.... March 10, 1915 we left our splendid city of Petrograd. All of her streets were piled with snowdrifts, and on Nevsky Prospect there were masses of people. But I remember how sad my soul was; I even shed tears for my dear homeland. Apparently my soul already felt then that something terrible awaited Russia. How many of those people, then young and happy, are no longer among the living?

In 1915 we, eleven missionaries, travelled across Romania, Bulgaria, Serbia and Greece, and, although it was during a horrible war, we saw God's churches everywhere; everywhere religious people prayed. In Thessalonica in the cathedral of the holy Great Martyr Dimitry, we prayed on Great Friday. We celebrated the Paschal night on the steamship. It was very rough, but we served Matins anyway. Oh, how sad it was; each of us remembered our native land, our families and friends. We all poured tears. On the first day of Pascha we landed in Piraeus, Greece [the port of Athens], and I was able to stand a little in church, having caught the end of Vespers.   [1943]

***

I served Vigil for the "Burial of the Mother of God," but I served, sang and read alone. In the church two old ladies prayed. But I remember what Bishop Appolinarius wrote me from New York when I was still in Afognak: "In my church three to four old ladies prayed." And on the eve of a great Feast of the Mother of God—Her Dormition! And in my church at that time in Afognak I had a full church!

On the feast day I served the Liturgy, and afterwards we drank tea under the trees. At 4:00 in the afternoon I served a moleben with an Akathist. It was a beautiful day, sunny, warm. After the moleben we prayed fervently for Russia and all Christian countries. At the ectenias

Afognak church at the time of Fr. Gerasim. His house is seen on the left.

Fr. Gerasim reads the Great Canon from Great Lent
in the midst of his Afognak flock.

I sent up a prayer to the Lord, not from the service book, no, but from my own heart and soul, conversing with the Lord. I said what was prompted to me by, as I believe, my heavenly friends, the Sufferers in the name of God.

The entire service was very solemn. I served enthusiastically; my voice sounded like a young man's. It is true my legs were tired. But glory to God and His Most Holy Mother for such mercy shown to me.

Ach, it is so hard to forget what it was like in Russia under the Tsars. In our Tula, in its Kremlin, there was also an ancient cathedral church of the Dormition, with a beautiful, tall bell tower. Its holy walls were all painted with excellent frescoes. There was also a tall, carved wood iconostasis. It was closed long ago. And the magnificent Kazan Cathedral stood not far from the Kremlin. A cathedral in the Byzantine style, that I so loved—long ago destroyed.

No, I cannot but grieve! But to whom shall I confess my grief? Only in prayer to God, to the Mother of God, to the holy God-pleasers, shall I, sinful monk Gerasim, reveal my heart and soul.   [1962]

16. The Quake of 1964

The calamity occured in Ouzinkie the night of the 27th of March, 1964. The water caught up with me not in the church house, but in the house of one parishioner, not far from the sea. Running up the hill, she forgot her purse with money and sent her father-in-law, V. Ponomarov, to bring it. I met him and went with him into the house. The water already began to flood the house. Looking for the purse I came into the bedroom, and returning into the kitchen I heard: "Father, we cannot get out, already the water is coming in." A frightful thing was there to be seen: the water poured in like a river. I got up on a chair, and the chair sunk under the water. Then on the table! I sat down and began to pray. The house was shaking with great force and everything was cracking. I expected the house to be washed into the sea, and I prayed!

I was bidding farewell to all. The water also covered the table. I remembered everything very clearly, and mentally was already in Russia and amidst my friends. That, what I experienced that moment, it is impossible to relate. I was already expecting my end, when I heard the voice of my friend in misfortune: "Father, do not be afraid, the water is leaving!" Rapidly the water was returning into the ocean. But everything around was frightful: The doors swung open, everything began to fall into the water and was being carried away by the water. I expected the house to collapse—it was raised off its foundation and was collapsing on one side. The steps with the porch were carred into the sea. We jumped to the ground. It was a frightful picture. If it were high tide and there were strong winds, we all would have perished.

All people were as if petrified. They ran in fear up the hill and for three days remained there. And then life began, as bad as before.

All the time the tremor continued and at times quite threatening. Our Island sunk nine feet. In some places the roads and pathways were washed away. It is not true that the churches were not harmed. In the Chinnik village the whole village was washed away, including the chapel. In Kachuv village on Kodiak island everything was washed away, including the new chapel. In Afognak village the water inundated the church, but it miraculously was preserved. Therein were beautiful icons, painted in the Kiev Caves Lavra, a gift of Patriarch Tikhon. There was also an icon from Mt. Athos of the Mother of God "Comfort and Consolation." [In this icon] the Mother of God looks as if alive. Her eyes penetrate into a human soul. I used to serve molebens and read akathists every day. I sorrowed for that temple of the Nativity of the Mother of God and prayed during that frightful night. Now they decided to move the whole village to Kizhyak. It is not far from Ouzinkie. I visited it, but long ago. I grieve over my beloved island—after all I lived in these places for forty-seven years. All people around became very nervous. After all, the tremor continued for a very long time, and the weather kept being stormy and cold. [It took place on Good Friday, according to the civil calendar.]

The two chapels in my hermitage, where Elder Herman rests, were not damaged as they are far from the sea. In the smaller chapel, where there are several objects of Elder Father Herman, even the oil in the lampadas was not spilled. Yes, that was a miracle: the humble kamilavka* of Elder Herman that was placed under a glass covering on a stand—remained in its place while all candles were knocked off of the candlestand.

The earthquake was pretty strong. The trees, those huge spruces, were bent low. In Ouzinkie the oil of all the lampadas was spilled. Even all the bells rang. It was a frightful picture, that terrible night. Remaining in my hermitage, I rarely would receive my mail.

My salvation was a miracle, since the house wherein I was, was raised by the tidal wave from its wooden pilings and carried into the sea. I believe someone was praying for me during those hours.

[February, 1965]

17. A Call to Start a Monastery on Spruce Island

Soon there will be 120 years since the repose of Elder Herman in Alaska. He was buried on Spruce Island. It is necessary to renovate the chapel there and to paint it. There is a need of a lampada. It is time to light a lamp with an eternal flame on the grave of our wonderworker. One wishes that there would be established a skete there. Perhaps some monks would be found, who would express the desire to come into this desert-dwelling place from their noisy cities. Perhaps there will be found some kind people who would be willing to organize a society or a brotherhood in the name of Father Herman of Alaska and to labor for this godly elder by finding means in order to fix the chapel and to erect a house for guests. The time flies fast and soon there will be 1957. One must only begin and the work will go by itself. It is good to have here

---

*It has now been taken by the Kodiak clergy to Kodiak, with St. Herman's relics.

a skete: the place is very suitable; it is deserted here. It is possible to build little cells in the woods and live one by one. With God's help everything is possible to achieve. In Alaska there must be a skete! The time has come when it is necessary to begin to serve daily Liturgy near the grave of Fr. Herman. St. Herman is waiting for monks. He prophesied that they will be on his New Valaam. The time is approaching in order to achieve this, hoping in the Lord God. That was his prophecy.

[*Russian American Orthodox Messenger,*
January, 1954]

* * *

....*And with God's grace a whole multitude of young penitent monastics are now conducting a full cycle of services as in Valaam, to the heavenly joy of St. Herman and Fr. Gerasim. On St. Herman's repose day, November 15/28, 1997, a renovated beach house building of two stories with a tower was built. From that day forward divine services have been served in the new tower-wing. Fr. Gerasim's descendants are taking on themselves all of his inheritance, both the joys and even the sorrowful persecutions that come from the Kodiak clergy, as in the time of St. Herman (✝ 1836) so also in the time of Archimandrite Gerasim (✝ 1969).*

The call of Father Gerasim still resounds and echoes in the hearts of modern-day humble God-seekers. God protect them through the prayers of St. Herman and Fr. Gerasim.

Archimandrite Gerasim, summer, 1961.
I photographed him on the day of the 100th anniversary of the
canonization of his favorite saint, Tikhon of Zadonsk.

Letters of Father Gerasim of Spruce Island to His Brotherhood

(to Abbot Herman, then Gleb Dimitrievich Podmoshensky)

"Relay my full prostration to all your beloved brethren. Oh, pray for me, my dear co-brothers."
—Archimandrite Gerasim

Young novice Michael (the future Fr. Gerasim) with his friend
the future Athonite Barsanuphius, officially photographed
in an Alexin studio, on the eve of his departure to Mt. Athos.

LETTER 1
May 30, 1961

My dear brother in Christ Jesus, Gleb,

The grace of God be with you. Your letter of the 24th of April I received in Ouzinkie Village on the 1st of May. You write to me that this summer you dream of visiting Spruce Island and the grave of Elder Father Herman. It is difficult for me to answer all your questions. The most important thing here is that many dollars are needed. Now all this travelling is done on airplanes, actually visiting all places. Of course it is possible to go by ship, wherever they go. From San Francisco to Seattle it is possible to travel either by plane, by sea, or by railroad. But from Seattle to Kodiak they don't go directly. And if they stop in the city of Seward, then one must wait for a small mail ship. In Kodiak and in Ouzinkie there are Orthodox people. But I must tell you that during the summertime all our people are fishing; they're busy, and it is difficult at times to find a ride by boat. Besides, the place where the boat lands, Monks' Lagoon, is very rough, and it is not always possible to get there at all times. Concerning your stay with me as a guest, you are welcome. But I must tell you that during summertime it is hard to get to me and to leave. In any case, one must be prepared to wait. It is difficult to say what kind of weather there will be. Last summer was rainy, cold, stormy, and rarely did I see people.

In former days, when I was younger, I spent the winter here in my desert. I would leave it for the Christmas holidays or during the days of Great Lent and Pascha. Keep in mind I am serving a parish in a little village, Ouzinkie. I cannot tell you how much time it will take to reach Spruce Island. I have never been in San Francisco and do not know how

87

much time it takes, even by plane. I was in Seattle in 1928. My desert hermitage is about seven or eight miles away from the village of Ouzinkie. From Kodiak in a motor boat it takes a bit more than an hour. My helper is a barely literate Aleut. The choir is not that great. Our summer is short, but sometimes we have good autumns. However, now nature has changed. Today is the second of May, and at night we had frost. Our Pascha was cold; there was a severe western wind.

But again I must tell you that I cannot answer all your questions because I do not know much. Besides, now I am old and sick. Life here is very difficult: people have begun to drink a lot; they become proud and disobedient. I used to write much to the "humble" bishops and to fellow priests. But they have a cold attitude toward me; they don't believe me. It's evident! I am already seventy-two years and six months. On the 4th of May of this year, 1961, will mark forty-six years of my service in the North American diocese. In Russia I lived for nine years in a monastery.

I am tired, my dear brother Gleb. Forgive me. May God protect you.

Yours,
A. Gerasim

LETTER 2
October 21/November 3, 1961

Dear Gleb Dimitrievich,

The mercy of God be with you. You left Spruce Island on the 15th/28th of August, and it is as if you drowned in the water—no news. On that day, August 15th, I was immersed in deep sorrow. From my childhood years I have not liked to part either with relatives or friends, for this was so sad for me. Moreover, those who came to me for the Dormition feast day did not come to church, but were drinking. And this feast day has been dearly beloved by me from my childhood years.

Each year my native Tula comes up in my memory with its wonderful church services on August 16th, when the burial service to the Mother of God takes place; its unforgettable solemn services, the singing of the huge chorus and the church packed with people. Oh, what took place there I shall never forget until my death. On the 17th there was a solemn Divine Liturgy and the grand cross procession with the shroud of the Mother of God around the church of the Protection of the Mother of God. But most of all, I loved, just like all our people of Tula, the wonderful service of the burial of the Mother of God. It is impossible to describe it—one must see and experience all that for oneself!

On the 7th of September something happened to me. I woke up and did not feel too good: in my ears there was a noise, in the back of my head a sharp pain, and my vision became different. I somehow see everything double. I thought that it was due to high blood pressure. Each year on the 25th of August (old style) I used to serve an All-night Vigil in the large chapel where there is an ancient icon of the Mother of God. But last year, I was forced to serve in the small chapel. And of course in it I served also to the Mother of God and to the martyrs [Adrian and Natalia]. But it was hard for me to read; something bothered me, and I couldn't see straight. But that is my old age; it is because I have become weak and sick.

With each delivery of mail I am expecting a letter from you. Today is already November 3rd, and still no news from you. You asked for a little icon. Forgive me, so far I don't have any old painted icons from Alaska. I looked all over. Whatever I have is in my cell. Thank you for leaving a photo of the weeping Iveron icon of the Mother of God. It is indeed very sorrowful that, for the last twenty-four years that I have lived here, no one was able to build a house here so that pilgrims can stay for a while and pray. My place is very small and it is difficult for me at such an age to receive visitors. There is a lot of work to be done, even for those who live in the desert. Now I can no longer work much—I have no strength and my legs have become weak—woe is me.

A letter came for you, sent from Los Angeles, California. Forgive me that I by mistake opened the first envelope, thinking that it was my letter. I am sending it back to the monastery.

Father Abbot Ambrose* returned to Canada to his desert hermitage. He wrote to me that he visited your monastery. He is older than me by six years and still visits various places. Not I, in such years I would have wished to stay in a monastic cell far away from the world. Oh, how good it is for a monk on the Holy Mountain of Athos!! This is the only place in the world which was chosen by the Heavenly Queen. I grieve over the fact that it is being abandoned by Constantinople and that the Athonite metochions, and their beautiful churches are empty.

I received a letter from Russia. Of course, there is not a word about church matters. They have to praise everything, that everything is fine and dandy there.

Poor, poor, Russian people.

Today is the 21st and I re-read your article, "The Image of Humility: A Hundred Years Since the Death of Optina Elder Macarius."** Optina Monastery and its elders have been known to me since my childhood years. I knew Father Archimandrite Xenophon well. I knew the nuns of the Shamordino Kazan Convent as well. I served an All-night Vigil [for the feast of the Kazan Icon] and mentally visited their churches and cathedrals that are dedicated in honor of the Kazan Icon of the Mother of God. In our town of Tula, there was a huge, beautiful Kazan Cathedral, and there was a miracle-working icon of the Mother of God. Now, all that has been destroyed and annihilated.

I still remember very well what you read to me on St. Tikhon of Zadonsk.*** What a meek, humble hierarch who had to endure so much in his much-sorrowing life. I was very saddened by the fact that they denied his serving of Liturgy and receiving of Holy Communion

---

*His father-confessor; see *Elder Ambrose of Optina*, St. Herman Press, Platina, California, 1997, pp.10-30.

** A chapter in *Optina Monastery and Its Era*, by I. M. Kontzevitch, N. Y., 1976.

***See the article on St. Tikhon of Zadonsk in *The Orthodox Word*, No. 13, 1966.

Fr. Gerasim's confessor Archimandrite Ambrose Konavalov,
a Canadian missionary.

for the last time: and they were even monks. On Mount Athos in our big Russian monasteries sick monks were given Communion every day. It was good there, there were churches next to infirmaries wherein they served daily the Divine Liturgy. In this case they refused to give Communion to a sick hierarch who was a holy man. I still cannot forget what you read in my cell. I told you that I venerated this hierarch from my youthful days. I am very glad that you helped me on the day of his jubilee and our service came out so beautifully. Glory be to God! And we were able to pray for those who bear his holy name and whom the Lord called to His heavenly abodes. I will not conceal that I would have been happy if they would have given me his name at my tonsure. But I love also the name of St. Gerasim of the Jordan River. Everything is from the Lord!

Today is the 22nd of October (old style). The day was beautiful! The sun was shining, it was not cold. I served Liturgy and a moleben to the Mother of God. Of course as always on such feast days I cannot avoid remembering my dear native land, our beautiful cathedral and churches. Alas, they do not exist any more. And that majestic Kazan Cathedral in Petrograd was turned into a museum of atheism.

Today I received the magazine *Orthodox Russia,* No. 18. I read there an article by Bishop Savva: "An Appeal to Priests." Bishop Savva surely writes well! But people today have developed cold and hardened hearts.

I hear the Greeks are now allowing those who desire the monastic life to go to Mount Athos. But will there be found any in our days who would desire it?! A certain writer, George Grebenshchikov, writes in the newspaper *Svet:* "In America there are few who would wish to dedicate themselves to the monastic life." Oh these worldly writers! Why do they break into that which is not their business! It sounds as if in our Russia people went to the monastery because they could not feed themselves! Nonsense!

In St. Tikhon's Monastery there were many monks and novices from the southern part of Russia, where peasants were very well off. Many of them were even wealthy. People went to the monastery because they had a calling. Lazy-bones would also go, but would soon leave or be kicked out. Not long before the revolution our monasteries became rich and well-ordered and began to experience a need of workers, so they had to hire lay people. Our lover of monks, Archbishop Nikon, later of Vologda, also wrote about that.

Not far from the city of Tula a fairly large but well-ordered monastery was located, where by 1909 there were over forty monks in the brotherhood. After that year, when they appointed a vicar-bishop as abbot—a scholar of sorts, but who did not like simple monks—the monastery began to dwindle in numbers; no one wanted to go there. In those years in Russia there were many poor people. No, it is not true that only the poor went to the monastery. I knew young, healthy novices who were good, labor-loving, had various skills and who, spending three or four years there, would leave the monastery and return to the world. I do not know what they said to the Abbot, but they would share with their co-brothers that they were tormented by fleshly passions. Of course, rather than sin in the flesh, such should marry. But those who remained in the monastery lived peacefully, labored, and lovingly accepted the monastic rank. However, there was a bad thing too in Russia—light-minded women would tempt handsome novices and monks. I used to know such fallen ones, who grieved very much over it and would shed copious tears of repentance. There were also faithful monks who loved holy monasteries and monastic brothers. There were also those who would fall low and sin, but then would return to their Father's house and live like ascetics and good monks. The reverse also happened: some good, humble ryassaphore monks, whom people expected to develop into exemplary monks or great hierarchs, would fall; trapped in the clutches of Satan, they would get drunk, fornicate, and return to the world. My soul used to grieve about such, and in my young years my kind Elder [Ioasaph] more than once would say, "Oh, Misha, do not judge such people, but pray for them. Misha, a horse walks on four legs and even then it stumbles, and we people have only two legs." Now, when half a century has passed since the day of my parting with my kind, wise, holy Elder, I already have forgotten much. Of course, I still do remember some things, but now in such times who will find similar monks! But we saw them, we heard from them only good, instructive things. And he, my dear Elder Ioasaph, was clairvoyant. I think that I told you about him already.

Today is the 23rd of October (old style). Tomorrow is the 24th—the commemoration of the Joy of All Who Sorrow Icon of the Mother of God. I again involuntarily go back to my dear Russia and see again that wonderful church in Petrograd, with a lovely chapel where there was a miracle-working icon of the Mother of God, The Joy of All Who Sorrow. I see both the holy icon and a mass of flickering, multi-colored lampadas. From early childhood, I loved the twinkling little holy fire.

> Before an old icon a lamplight is flickering,
> Throwing a shadow on a ceiling so low,
> Thought after thought, bitter thoughts bickering,
> Now with each other of times long ago.

> How I remember her standing so tenderly,
> Clasping her hands, barely hiding her fears,
> Over my sick bed, she prayed so motherly,
> The icon light trembling in each of her tears.

A Poem by Nikitin

Well, I remembered much, and a tear ran down from my eyes. It seemed that it was so recently when I prayed in that beautiful chapel. I remember everything so clearly!!! And remembering this, involuntarily these words came from my lips: "O Lord, for what reason do we suffer so much, already for forty years?" Forgive me, O Lord, for such a question, but I find it hard to endure that calamity of my country, the suffering of our holy Church, the suffering of the Russian people. At times I can't even sleep at all during the whole night, and now everywhere there is debauchery, fighting, foul language, and fornication—it becomes even more difficult.

I grieve very much about the fact that I cannot remain in my desert all the time. When Elder Herman lived and labored here, there was a little settlement. People lived there. In those days people were different. They were obedient, they believed in God. But it is true that in those times the kind Elder Father Herman endured much also. It is also true that not all Aleuts loved him and helped him.

I sent a letter to Father Protopresbyter Adrian. I found out about him another new thing—that he was ordained into the priesthood by the former bishop of Tula and Belov, Parthenius. I also have his photograph. He was a simple and kind hierarch. No one writes to me from Tula any longer.

I'm sending my greetings to all the monks of the Holy Trinity Monastery, and I ask for their holy prayers. I also pray for them, both in my cell and in the church. I rejoice over the blossoming of their holy monastery. Did you meet Patriarch Benedict? I am sorry and angry that he does not allow our bishops to serve in the Holy City! But I commemorate him at proskomedia, taking out a portion for each Orthodox Patriarch.

Forgive me, I don't write too well. My eyes grow dim, I cannot read or write for very long. But what can we do; everything is going that way.

Today is the 7th of November [new style]. It is chilly, damp, and there is a cold wind. It is not joyful. What kind of weather do you have at your place?

I'm expecting my mail. I haven't seen newspapers for quite a while, but it is true that there is nothing good in them. Hieromonk Father Cyril was transferred to Sitka. I wonder who was appointed to Juneau. Stay healthy and may God protect you.

A. Gerasim

LETTER 3
May 17, 1962

The book on Elder Hieroschemamonk Joseph is very well written, it is very touching! I read it with deep reverence. You know I lived in those places more than five years and knew many of them and the abbots of those monasteries, and both monks and nuns, too. It was a grace-filled diocese! The diocese was occupied by a hierarch of high monastic life. One of its first Archpastors was Hierarch Philaret* [of Kiev], a true monastic and lover of monastics. He founded the Skete of the Forerunner near Optina Monastery and invited good ascetic monks there. There were also other hierarchs of holy life on the Kaluga Cathedra.

There were also wonderful monasteries and a monastery of St. Tikhon of Kaluga; but what was bad about it there was that it was too close to a huge village, and the world would rush into the monastery. Nearby there was a skete dedicated to the Meeting of the Lord, about six miles from the monastery. But its silence and seclusion were disturbed when they built a railroad nearby and even a station: "St. Tikhon's Hermitage." In that skete several great monastics worked out their salvation. One of them was Hieromonk Moses, a monk of holy life who kept a vow of silence, a semi-recluse. He was tortured by the Bolsheviks during the first years of the cruel Revolution. I wrote about him and about Elder Zosima, who was burnt to death in his forest cell, to Father Archpriest Michael Polsky, but for some reason he did not print it in his second volume.** I wrote of them only what my friend-monks wrote to me, about how they suffered for the name of God. But I knew them well myself while living in St. Tikhon's Monastery. Fr.

---

*Now canonized.

**New Martyrs of Russia, Vol. I (Jordanville, New York: Holy Trinity Monastery, 1946) and Vol II (Holy Trinity Monastery, 1957).

A pre-revolutionary postcard. "Greetings from St. Tikhon's Monastery," 1913. Such paintings would evoke longing in pilgrims to endure hardships on the way to monasteries.

А popular icon print of St. Tikhon of Kaluga,
showing his life as a dendrite in the forests of Kaluga.

A chapel built over St. Tikhon's oak, in which he lived for years.
Pre-revolutionary photo; all this is destroyed today.

St. Tikhon's monastery pond.

Тихонова Пустынь. № 2.
Спасо-Преображенскій соборъ.

Entrance to the Holy Transfiguration Cathedral.

General view of St. Tikhon's Monastery. In the center is the infirmary where Fr. Gerasim had his obedience as a novice.

The infirmary as it looks today, where services are conducted by the monks of the renewed monastery.

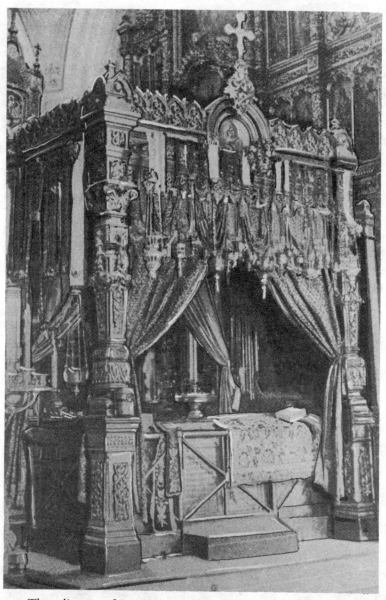

The reliquary of St. Tikhon in the Transfiguration Cathedral,
which was leveled to the ground by the communists.

Тихонова-Пустынь.
Успенскій храмъ и Св. ворота

St. Tikhon's Monastery: Dormition Church, belfry and main gate.

Zosima was the kindest elder; he loved to remember things from the past and how they were poor and simple during his early years there. Then everyone lived very amiably; there was more Christian love between brothers. The young novices loved him very much, and when he would come to the monastery from his faraway forest cell, they all would invite him to tea and the sweet talk would last until midnight. But his talk was not empty talk. No! That simple Elder would tell the young novices what should be the main work for young novices—obedience. He told much about his long monastic life, and everything he said taught each one to be kind, good, and obedient. Among them there used to be simple people, illiterate; there were wise, discerning monk-elders. Another recluse was Hieromonk Moses. He was an angel of God in the flesh. I do not know why the respectable Archpriest Michael Polsky did not mention these luminaries whom I described. The new Hieromartyr Bishop Nikodim did a great service while laboring in this grace-filled corner of Russia where there were many wondrous ascetics, about whom he gathered much good information and recorded it all. I deeply revere Bishop Nikodim and the ascetics of Kaluga. While reading about Elder Joseph it seemed to me that I mentally visited that grace-filled part of Holy Russia.

You know, I had just decided to order this book, and suddenly I received it from you. May the Lord save you!

Yesterday, from the 28th to the 29th, the whole night I had pain in my chest and couldn't sleep. Oh, pray for me, my dear co-brothers.

Yours truly and loving you,
A. Gerasim

LETTER 4
October, 1962

Dear in Christ Jesus, Br. Gleb!

May God protect you!

Forgive me for my lengthy silence. I could not write, and have not written all summer. I returned from Kodiak at the end of the fourth week of the holy Great Fast and began to serve. In Kodiak I was ill the entire time. I wasn't doing any better when I returned to Ouzinkie. Gene [Sundberg] did not come to visit me on Spruce Island. He has an addition to the family, and he could not come. Furthermore, his foreman flew to Chicago, and he is very busy. We had a nice summer; it was sunny. But few people visited me. There were a lot of fish; everyone was busy. Afterwards, at the end of August, they began to drink and carouse, to spend money on flights—some to Seattle and others to Anchorage. Many have already gone astray.

I stayed in the hermitage from May 30th to September 11th. But every day I did not feel well. With shortness of breath and great difficulty I cleaned the chapel and swept the walkway. But I served everyday. I served forty-two Liturgies. I could not sleep. I would wake up early and go to the chapel. I love to commemorate the souls of the departed, and God gave me strength. On the Feast of the Dormition of the Mother of God, I served the entire service by myself without omission. There were pilgrims—three old ladies. But the men, the Aleuts, were drunk.

There is something wrong with my eyes. The quarrel in San Francisco disturbed me. It really disturbed me! I even served the service to the Iveron Icon of the Mother of God.

Fr. Macarius Targansky is still in Kodiak. During Great Lent on Wednesdays and Fridays he served the [Presanctified] Liturgy in the evenings. This is some "novelty" for me.

I pray for you, for your mother Nina, and for your sister, too. I also commemorated those whose names you left on the list. I remember you also for your labor of cutting grass. Alas, I could not do this even during the last summer. But soon I will be seventy-four years old. Oh, it has become hard for me to live here. People drink and carouse; there is shooting at night. After Pascha I was so frightened that I got into bed. One drunk man came to greet me and went into the general store [in Ouzinkie] and said there, "Father Gerasim is sick; he can't talk. I think he has had a stroke." Well, a clamor arose, and they announced this on the radio [CB]. Many were frightened, and most of all Gene. He flew in to see me and spent the night with me. Well, forgive me, I can't write anymore.

Relay my full prostration to all your beloved brethren.

May the Lord protect you.

Your A[rchimandrite] Gerasim

I am sending you holy water and earth. [From St. Herman's spring and grave.]

LETTER 5
October 30 (n.s.), 1962
To Fr. Vladimir in Jordanville and to Br. Gleb

Holy Fathers!

Forgive me for my mistake! I at first received a package of books I did not order, and a bill for them. Then I thought that it was some sort of mistake, which sometimes happens. So yesterday on October 29th I wrote to you a letter and was about to go to the post office, but something prevented me and I decided: "Well, tomorrow is the 30th. I will get up earlier and go to the post office."

In the evening I read for a long time the book on Elder Father Joseph [of Optina]. It is hard to tear oneself from it, and especially for me, who knew those places from childhood and loved them. This morning on the 30th of October something again prevented me from going, and I again took up the book about Elder Joseph and read it, forgetting that I had to go to the post office. Suddenly, a knock on the door. I came out and saw a young girl bringing me my mail. And what do you think? Thus I received all I asked you to send me. I was very glad to receive the akathist to St. Seraphim of Sarov! Mine is already old, it was hard to hold in my hands. The book is wonderful, the type large. I thank you, and also for everything that you sent me. Three copies of the Prayer Book are also wonderful.

I received No. 19 of the journal *Orthodox Russia* with its supplement. There is the magazine *Orthodox Life*. I read the creation of Gleb D. Podmoshensky: "Missionary Exploit." He asked me to write something about Elder Herman, but from the end of April of 1962 until the middle of September I did not write to any one, because I simply could not write! Just the same, what he asked me I could not write to him. I do not know where the disciple of Elder Father Herman, Sophia, was buried and where she lived. No one knows either what kind of icon of the Mother of God it was which Father Herman placed on the seashore and said: "The water will not rise higher than this!" Bishop Philip Stavitsky, who visited the hermitage at the end of June, 1917, wanted very much to know about it. But alas, no one knew about it here. Besides, much was taken away or stolen from the little chapel. Bishop Alexey Panteleev kept records about Elder Father Herman. He managed to collect quite a list, concerning help to those who asked Fr. Herman. But he, although considered by the "Platonites" as a meek and humble man, was far from being such. He knew nothing about monasticism and Orthodox monasteries. I was quite amazed when he visited Spruce Island in May of 1936 and, entering the little chapel where a copy of the Kaluga Icon of the Mother of God is located on the eastern wall, asked me: "What kind of an icon is it anyway? I never saw such a one. And why is she painted without the infant?" I told him: "This is the Kaluga Mother of God and is well known in many of our churches and all over Russia." He told me once again: "No, I never saw such a one before!"

Leaving Alaska, he should have submitted that report to those who entrusted him to complete it. It belongs to the North American diocese. Yes! Such a thing is very sad! But then, when he was collecting information here about the Elder, about his miracles that the believing people received at his grave, then there were still many old people alive. Now they are all dead. In Afognak there lived a very old lady, Babushka Paraskeva,* who still remembered that Sophia.

Now, having written this, my eyes have become tired. It is hard for me to write. Nevertheless, I'm sending you dollars, and you know yourself the price of all you sent me.

Thank you and forgive me.

A. Gerasim

LETTER 6
November 6th (n.s.), 1962

Your honor, Gleb Dimitrievich!

I'm sending you greetings from cold Alaska! Your letter (without a date) was received by me on November 5th, new style. And also three little icons. No, your letter with questions was indeed received by me. But then I could not write and did not write to anyone. I could not decipher your address then. To write at the address of the monastery to "Br. Gleb" is one thing, but to write like that outside of it is somewhat awkward, or that is what I think. When I lived in the monastery in Russia, then people wrote to me: to Novice Michael Schmaltz. But when I would be on leave for a longer time, then my monk-friends wrote to me: to Michael Alexandrovich Schmaltz. Before tonsure into

---

*Or, Babushka Pelagia, vividly described in a recent book *Derevnia's Daughters* by Lola Harvey, 1992.

Babushka Pelagia Grigorieff.

Ryassaphore we were addressed as Brother. And in some monasteries they did not change the name even after the tonsure into the ryassa!

What icon Elder Herman brought out on the seashore during the high rising of the water is not known. Back in 1917, Bishop Philip Stavitsky, visiting Kodiak, Afognak, Ouzinkie, and Woody Island in the month of July, asked many of the old people about that. But alas, none of them knew anything about it.

Basil Skvortzoff [once] fell into an open hold on a fishing schooner in Kodiak and badly hurt his shoulder on the cement bottom. Returning home to Ouzinkie, he suffered from pain for several days. In those days there was not a doctor in Kodiak, and people would be treated with home remedies. But others, more religious people, would turn with prayer to God, to the Mother of God, to God's saints. So Basil Skvortzoff got into his boat and went to the grave of Father Herman.

At that time it was not possible to get under the church; everything was closed up and only on the eastern side of the chapel was there a hole cut out. People would stretch their arms through that opening and take earth from the grave. So Basil did the same. He stuck his hand into the hole, took some earth, and, uncovering his shoulder and arm and pronouncing, "Well, Old Man, I came to you; help me," rubbed the afflicted spot with earth from Father Herman's grave. The pain at once disappeared, and he returned home quite healthy. Many old people used to tell about wondrous miracles that took place on the grave of Fr. Herman and everywhere in Alaska when believing people had recourse to him with prayer. I cannot write much now; my eyesight has become worse. Soon I'll be 74 years old.

In the biographies of the Optina Elders, of both Fr. Ambrose and Fr. Joseph, Hieromonk Clement Sederholm, the son of a German pastor, is mentioned, about how he was a man of rare sincerity and a lofty, noble soul, an ascetic who would fulfill his monastic rules with all precision. But at the same time he possessed an extremely emotional temper and excessive, typically German precision. He couldn't get along with a single novice. Fr. Clement suffered with that, repented, and confessed to the elder, humbly bowing down and begging forgiveness of the novices, but he could not conquer this impatience at all. But Fr. Joseph came out in this case a victor. About him Fr. Clement used to say: "Fr. Joseph is the only person at whom I cannot get angry; I don't even know how to get irritated with him." But were there many such lucky people?!

Abbess of Mount Athos

Do you think that the "Platonites" think or care about our ascetic Elder Herman?!! No, and No! The Platonites did not allow Bishop Ambrose to make a collection throughout the whole Metropolia to repair the Sitka Cathedral, saying: "No, no, we have many of our own needs!" Bishop Ambrose himself told me that. In America in our diocese the white clergy did not like monks, even before the Revolution. Besides, some hierarchs used to be secular priests. Bishop Alexey Panteleev knew absolutely nothing about the monastic life, about our monasteries, even about such a luminary as St. Seraphim of Sarov, about whom he read for the first time only in 1938, spending a month on Spruce Island. I gave him at that time this book to read.... And he said he had studied in a Theological Seminary and a year in the Academy.

You were in the chapel here on Spruce Island and you saw that wonderful icon of the Mother of God, "Abbess of Holy Mount Athos." Bishop Alexey had a cold reaction to it; not once did he venerate it. I told him then: "I ordered such an icon to be painted because the Mother of God is the abbess of monastics—She is our Defendress. And just like on Mount Athos, when intending to serve I pray to Her; I beg a blessing of Her." To this he answered me: "This is on Athos and nowhere else!" Then I told him what the Mother of God told Elder Father Hieroschemamonk Parthenius of Kiev, and also what the blessed Novice Thecla heard, who slept for twenty and a half hours after receiving Holy Communion and much was shown to her of the life beyond the grave, and how the holy Great Martyr George said: "Pray

"New Valaam" Icon of the Theotokos of Mt. Athos,
in the main chapel at Monks' Lagoon, painted on Mt. Athos in
the 1940's specifically for Fr. Gerasim and New Valaam.

to Her, pray always. She is the Defendress for all Christians. Day and night She prays before Her Son and God, and She prays for monks especially, so that they will not put to shame Her robes, which they wear...."

People have become so cold to such a holy thing!

Dedicating One's Life to St. Herman

You write that you have developed great love and faith in Elder Herman and that you are thinking of dedicating your life to him somehow. Well, pray to God and our Protectress, the Mother of God, to Sts. Herman, Seraphim, and others. I also, preparing to go to Spruce Island, fervently prayed to them. Yes, at that time the whole malicious power of the "Platonites" armed itself against me. Oh, how hard it was for me, how I suffered. But the Lord helped me; Elder Herman received me kindly. And now I have been living here for twenty-seven years. Should I be telling others about what you are thinking? There is no one to tell here. Who here can understand such a thing?! Alas, even here it is difficult to live now. People are going crazy; they have forgotten God! Oh, it is hard!!! Often, quite often, I do not sleep at night. I cannot be healthy again, "As for the days of our years, in their span they be threescore years and ten. And if we be in strength, mayhap fourscore years; and what is more than these is toil and travail" (Ps. 89:10-11). And such ailments and pain—have begun now.

St. Seraphim

The weather here is now wet, cold, and stormy.

Recently I received a letter from Mount Athos. It's bad there. They write to me that in St. Elias Skete there are no longer daily liturgies. In St. Andrew's Skete, where there used to be more than 500 monks in 1911-12, now the abbot himself serves every day, Father Archimandrite Michael. In the monastery of Holy Great Martyr Panteleimon there are five hieromonks, three hierodeacons. All of this saddens me. Now I often call to St. Seraphim: "O Holy Father Seraphim, our joy, pray to

God for us, who languish in a foreign land, and for our poor unfortunate suffering homeland—Russia!"

Yes, I often repeat St. Seraphim's testament.* Of course we cannot
get to his grave in order to tell him all that grieves us all these long years.
But I have preserved his little icon, which was unexpectedly given to me
as a gift in 1906 in the month of July, during the first month of my life
in the monastery of St. Tikhon, Wonderworker of Kaluga, by a young
Theodore. I remember clearly up to now how I then rejoiced over such
a gift. And since that day it has been inseparably with me. It was with
me on Mount Athos and it came with me to America and Alaska.

"Missionary Harvest"

Today is the feast day of the icon of the Mother of God "Joy of All
Who Sorrow." And yesterday, the 5th of November (new style) in the
evening I read the akathist to Her and an akathist to St. Seraphim. The
monastery published a new akathist to him, for which I am very glad.
Mine is falling apart. New type—wonderful. In the 10th issue of
Orthodox Life I also read your article, "Missionary Exploit." Yes, indeed,
we all must pray: the harvest is ready and the workers are few. O Lord,
send workers for Thy harvest!...

Yes, there were times in Holy Russia when for the post of hierarch
they would elect monks from our monasteries, but monks of holy life,
well-read, wise, intelligent; and they would bring tremendous good
both for the Church of Christ and for their flock. But, of course in our
time a hierarch should be an Orthodox man, educated and of righteous
life, who knows well Holy Scripture. Forgive me. I'm sending greetings
to your close ones. May Christ protect you.

Your A. Gerasim

P.S. I sent a little package to the monastery because I thought that you
would already be there.

---

*"When I am no more, come to my grave...."

LETTER 7
November 13, 1962

Your honor, Gleb Dimitrievich,

May the mercy of God be with you!

Your letter of November 8th was received by me in Ouzinkie on the 13th of November, new style.

Right now I cannot remember the year when Basil Skvortzoff fell into the hold of his schooner. It was long ago; I was still living in Afognak. But I think it must have been thirty-five years ago.

Another case was told to me by Emilian Petelin, how a certain woman had terribly painful births. I also do not remember now her name or family name. Being pregnant once again and suffering terribly, not long before giving birth she decided to go to Elder Herman's grave. They could not go by boat because around the east side there was a storm. So they went by way of Pestrikoff Beach, from where you also attempted to reach me on foot. Even for a healthy woman such a walk is not an easy one. There are no roads there, just a narrow path and in places streams, swamps, actually tundra. But she walked all the way and arrived safely; all went well. They (she and her husband and someone else) prayed, drank some water from the spring, and took some earth from the Elder's grave. They returned the same way on foot to the beach and reached home. And, O the wonder! The same night she gave birth without any pain! That was in 1927.

There was another case. A Creole woman, Alexandra Charalampievna Wotch, suffered from asthma and severe headache. When government ships would come to Kodiak with doctors aboard, she would go to them with her ailments. She would take various medicines, but they did not help her. Once she decided to visit the grave of Elder Herman. She got there without any difficulty; her asthma did not bother her. Having prayed there at the grave of Elder Herman, she

The Petelin family, Emilian's wife Maria, her maiden name Wotch.
Her mother Alexandra Charalampievna, who saw St. Herman as a girl
and was buried by Fr. Gerasim, is here seated in a black dress.
Picture taken in Cooke Inlet.

Fr. Gerasim's friend,
Michael Z. Vinokouroff.

Dr. Nelson, of Nelson Island,
whom Fr. Gerasim received into
Orthodoxy before his death.

drank some water, took some earth, and returned home to Kodiak, where she never again suffered from shortness of breath! She died in Afognak and I served her funeral.

Her maiden name was Alexandra Charalampievna Ilarionova, but her married last name was Wotch. She told me the following: "Our mother would always tell us: 'Children, pray to God for the Tsar. Pray more often. It will be bad when there will no longer be in Russia an Orthodox Tsar! Pray to Appa Herman. After that there will be bad times in Alaska; all kinds of seducers of various faiths will arrive here in Alaska and will seduce us. It will be bad here also! Pray for the Russian Tsar that God protect him and his family.'"

Other similar things old believing people used to tell me. There were righteous people here, too. Here is what Emilian Ivanovich Petelin told me about how his grandmother died. Emilian then was a young man and used to work in a store in Kodiak. Once an acquaintance of his came to his store and said: "Emilian, your grandmother wishes to see you at once." He went home and the old lady said to him: "Sit down, Emilian, I want to talk to you! I will die today and now I want to ask you to believe in God and to stay Orthodox your whole life. I raised you Orthodox and I ask you: do not change your Orthodox faith. And also: do not go to the States where there are no Orthodox people." But Emilian began to cry, begging her to bless him to go to the States in order to get an education. And only for that, and not too willingly, did she give her blessing. And then his grandmother indeed died that very evening.

Yes, a lot could have been gathered of a good, truthful and useful nature even from our cold Alaska, once belonging to our Russia. And it would have been better here if in 1907 Archbishop Platon Rozhdestvensky had not been sent to America. It was he who in 1909 closed the Sitka Seminary and Orphanage. And also the same in Unalaska. Alaska was abandoned by them. Bishop Alexander Nemolovsky only carried the title of being bishop of Alaska; he did not even visit his Alaskan diocese. Neither did Archbishop Platon visit

Alaska. And when Bishop Philip Stavitsky was appointed here, by that time World War I had broken out, times were bad, and in Alaska everything was in neglect—everything was falling apart. The Sitka Cathedral was in a pitiful state. The roof was leaking, the floor fallen in. The bishop's house was a total mess. Bishop Philip, young, energetic and talented, looking at all that would shed tears, and, looking at the portrait of Hierarch Metropolitan Innocent, he would say: "Forgive them, O great hierarch and apostle, for they have abandoned all your labors; they think only about earthly glory, a rich diocese! Forgive, if it is possible to forgive them for that!" At the end of July, 1917, he went to Russia by way of Japan to attend the All-Russian Council, where he decided to tell the truth about the Alaskan diocese. But God did not bless him to return here. The Bolsheviks did not allow him.

I thank your mother, the handmaiden of God, Nina, for the desire to help me. I am an old man, a sick old man, and I do not need much. Better help those who are in need. On the 10th of November, old style, I turned seventy-four.

Thank you. I sent you the water; I always pray for you both in the church and in my cell. I send greetings to Mrs. Nina Podmoshensky and to Ia.

In the Monastery of Great Martyr Panteleimon [on Mt. Athos] I stayed for some time and prayed in October, 1911. Since then fifty-one years have passed by. I knew Archimandrite Justinian only from his photographs, but Father Hierodeacon Philip I do not know. But I know their famous Archimandrite Cyricus; he had a wonderful voice, a bass. In those days he liked to drink, yet he was a simple, kind man. But that was so long, long ago; all of them have gone to the other world. Such a beautiful iconostasis made me a little sad. And such wonderful vestments on the father-monks.

The rain pours down, the sea roars. It's only fifteen minutes after three, and it's already dark. Forgive me.

Yours in spirit,
A. Gerasim

The glorious Athonite Archimandrite Cyricus.

LETTER 8
November 15/28, 1962
To Br. Alexander Pernits*

Most respected Alexander Vladimirovich!

May God's mercy be with you!

Your letter of November 11/24 was received by me on 14/27. Today, the 15th/28th, is the day of the repose of Elder Father Herman. A Russian man, a son of Archpriest Zenobius Vinokouroff, Michael Zinovievich Vinokouroff, working in the Congressional Library in Washington D.C., discovered in metric (record) books that Father Herman died, not on December 13/26, as it was written and is being written, but on the 15th/28th of November, 1836.

In Kodiak, having found out about his death, people began to prepare for him a coffin, but the villagers of Spruce Island were ordered to wait for the authorities. However, that was against the will of Elder Father Herman himself, who asked the villagers not to inform them in Kodiak about his death, for his wish was that he be buried by the inhabitants of that settlement [in Monks' Lagoon]. But the authorities in those days were harsh, and the villagers were afraid to fulfill the wish of their kind Appa. A frightful storm rose up, which lasted for a long time. A long time passed by, and a coffin was sent in which the Elder was buried. The coffin was well made, it was covered with black fabric on the outside, on which were crosses made of gold galoon. Inside the lining was white. All this was clearly seen when I took out his relics. In the book published by Valaam it is written that the burial of Elder Herman took place a month after his repose. So you see they made a mistake; it was his burial that took place on December 13/26. Starting in 1936, I have been serving Liturgy for him on the 15th/28th of

---

*A friend of mine who wrote to Fr. Gerasim on my behalf, a seminarian.—A. H.

November. I serve at night the Liturgy of St. James the Brother of the Lord.

The Chapel Over His Grave

The chapel over the grave of Elder Herman was built according to the instructions of Archbishop Nicholas Zernov. He donated quite a large sum for it. But it is sad that it was not taken care of. It is true that the kindest priest, Batiushka Father Tikhon Shalamov, during his years of serving in Kodiak, watched over it for ten years. At his own expense he kept there a kind old Aleut who looked after the chapel and kept a lamp burning on the place of his repose, where a little shrine was built adorned with icons. In 1905, Fr. Tikhon Shalamov left Alaska and returned to Russia, to Vologda, in order to give his children an education. He was the kindest man, a wonderful administrator and talented preacher. After his departure, the Spruce Island Hermitage, the grave of Elder Father Herman, remained in neglect. In 1927, on May 14/27, I visited Spruce Island and was shocked at what I saw there!

In Russia before the Revolution people were able to freely gather donations for the repair of the chapel and for the upkeep of its icons, candlestands, lamps. And if the war had not occurred, and the Revolution, then I would have obtained from Russia porcelain glass lamps. Such lamps are suitable for the damp Alaska climate. The old-timers here used to say that the chapel used to be adorned with icons, and many of them had silver rizas. There also used to be large candlestands. But I did not see them there any longer.

Oh, how wonderfully in Russia the faithful people used to keep the graves of their righteous ones, the people chosen by God who prayed for us sinners. And especially were our nuns distinguished in this respect; they loved to do that and were artists of all sorts.... In 1908 in the St. Tikhon's Monastery, Schema-Hierodeacon Jerome died at the end of January. He used to tell me: "I know that we all must die, but I would wish to live just ten years more. But no, I know I am living out my last days." I remember him now, and I think that the Lord knows what He does for us. Were he to have lived ten years more, it would have been 1918, the most horrible year for monasteries and monastics. In that very year all monasteries were closed, and all monastics were banished. They did not spare even the old and sick. They left in the infirmary a 90-year-old Schemamonk, Ioasaph, a man of holy life, clairvoyant; even he was starved to death. The son of a priest, he had graduated with honors from the Tula Theological Seminary. He prepared us monks for these sorrowful years some three or four years in advance. Yes, we too are to blame for much. St. Tikhon's Monastery was a rich, well-to-do monastery, very beautiful. But what hurt it was the fact that a huge village was nearby. Summer nights on holidays women with fellows would conduct songs; one could hear the music. There were cases when young novices would fall. And often they were good men who, were it not for the village, would have been good monks. But those who got married, being already ryassaphore monks, were all unfortunate people. Some ended their lives quite tragically. I felt very sorry for such ones. Optina Monastery, on the contrary, was cut off from the world. Fortunate was that monastery or skete which was located far away from villages and towns. Of course, the enemy does his evil work everywhere; not even a desert will save one from him.

In May of 1911, Elder Joseph of Optina died, and in August, after Dormition, I left my unforgettable St. Tikhon's Monastery. Yes, I knew the Optina fathers Archimandrites Xenophon and Benedict. The Kaluga diocese was rich in monasteries and ascetics.

We have bad weather: storms, rain, snow, and it is damp. It is hard for an old sick man.

Your name, Alexander, I have already been commemorating in my prayers. You are still a student, you yourself need money, and why are you sending it to me? One can pray without money. I also pray for slave-of-God, Gleb and his mother Nina and sister Ia.

Today is a happy day for me, I served liturgy. It is a wonderful liturgy, that of the Holy Apostle James! Its prayers are so touching. So appropriate are they for our times! And indeed what terrible times we have now. In *New Dawn* I read that the Soviets decorated Patriarch Alexey with some award. What more could you ask! Archbishop Nikon, formerly of Vologda, not long before the First World War wrote in spiritual journals that the chest of a bishop or a presbyter should be decorated by a panagia and a pectoral cross only. That's absolutely right!!! The former bishop of Tula and Belyov, Laurence, himself a kind elder, a pious man, wrote in his Report to the Synod in 1906 that all these secular decorations, medals, which are hung upon clergy, must be laid aside, for there were not any upon the chests of the apostles. He also said that the chest of a bishop should be adorned by a panagia and a cross. And the chest of a priest—by a cross. But how is it possible for an Orthodox hierarch to receive awards from persecutors of Christ and His Holy Church?! From blasphemous, wicked defamers of God, of Christ our Savior, and the Mother of God?! Awards from cruel persecutors, torturers of Christians, millions of them?!! And he is already an old man of 80, soon going to the judgment of God!

On November 8/22 at twenty minutes past 2 a.m. we had a terrible subterranean explosion. The house where I live was all shaking, all quivering. But it was not an earthquake. It does happen when the earth opens up, cracks up! We live on a rather small island where occasionally there is a high rise of water. To a lesser degree earth tremors took place also on the 22nd at 2 p.m. People sin and fear nothing. What insensitivity on behalf of contemporary people, what coldness towards God, towards the Church of God. Even the children become angry, fresh and disobedient.

I also sorrow for Athos. What will happen if the prayer of righteous ones will stop?!! Elder Schemamonk Silouan used to say: "The world cannot exist without prayers for it by holy people; calamities will begin." And they already have begun. O Lord, forgive us! But all is in God's hands!

For a long time now I haven't received any letters from Russia. Only my sister writes me anyway. Summer here was a cold one this year, it rained until July. Vegetables did not grow much; there was no sun for them. The Lord is humbling the foolish. But I feel sorry for the people; they have suffered here since 1914. I serve molebens to the Mother of God and read akathists every Sunday and each feast day, also to St. Seraphim. I am very glad that the monastery published an akathist to him. My copy grew old, all worn out. Well, enough. Forgive me!

May Christ keep you! I am sending greetings to Brother Gleb, to Mrs. Nina Podmoshensky, and to Ia.

Yours in spirit,
A. Gerasim

LETTER 9
February 4, 1963

Dear Gleb Dimitrievich,

May the mercy of God be upon you. Thank you for your kind letter. In the *Orthodox Life* [in Russian] I read your article.* Concerning the blessed repose of Elder Father Herman on November 15/28, I was informed by Michael Zinovievich Vinokouroff, who previously worked in the library in Washington, D.C. In the book on Elder Herman it was printed that Elder Father Herman forbade the inhabitants of the settlement on Spruce Island to inform [the authorities in Kodiak] about his death, and he told them how he should be dressed and buried. The times were severe, and the Aleuts were afraid to bury the Elder without having informed those living in Kodiak, and therefore they sent a baidarka there. But everything came about the way Elder Father Herman wanted, who suffered so much from those authorities. A storm rose up and continued for a long time, just as it was written, and it stormed about a month. The feast day of Christmas was approaching, and it was dangerous for the priest to leave Kodiak and

---

*On Sergius Yanovsky, before whose grave Fr. Gerasim used to light a lampada in St. Tikhon's Monastery, while he was a novice there from 1906 to 1911.

his parishioners without church services on such a great feast day. During December the storm subsided. The Kodiak authorities sent a coffin to Spruce Island for Elder Father Herman. The coffin was made out of spruce boards, crafted by knowledgeable hands; the boards were smoothly planed. Outside the coffin was covered with black fabric and inside with white. There were crosses made out of gold galoon of Russian workmanship.* And the inhabitants of the Spruce Island settlement, having received the coffin, did everything as they were instructed by their beloved Abba Herman. In those days in Alaska there were severe winters, and I think it was difficult for the Aleuts to dig a grave where tall spruces grew. The coffin of Elder Herman was not buried deep at all. The earth was soft and loose. I did not even open it; all the bones I took out from the right side.

When I got underneath the chapel I was struck by what a pitiable state everything there was in. On the grave of Elder Herman old rotten beams had been thrown. There was no earthen mound. There were beams all over, old chips from old rotten crosses. Then I prayed and began to clear up everything there. The old beams are still today located near the chapel. At that time I cut out in the wall of the foundation a space and made a window near the grave of Elder Herman, erected a cross there, and hung a lampada. The chapel itself was in great neglect and was actually falling apart.

In 1936 the Council of Bishops appointed Bishop Alexey Panteleev, a former lay priest, to be the builder of a monastery. I know well that he gathered donations to build that monastery to the sum of more than $3,000, but of that not a single cent was spent for good useful work.

And what could I have done about it? The powerful weight of the Platonites was on his side. And when Bishop Alexey saw that nothing could come out of his intentions to build a monastery, then he tried to

---

*These details prove that the coffin in which he was buried came from Kodiak and was not made by the orphans on Spruce Island.

chase me out of Spruce Island, offering me several parishes. But I was not tempted. After Bishop Alexey, the Platonites consecrated a muzhik, John Zlobin. And he began to drive me out and wanted to put his own man, Sergei Irtel on Spruce Island. Although I did not ask anyone to defend me, the inhabitants of Kodiak interceded for me and gathered more than 250 signatures, but I, no matter what, would not leave my dear hermitage. Oh, how mean are some "humble" bishops! Now twenty-eight years and four months have passed, and I am still guarding the grave of my loving Elder Father Herman. And tell me: whom did human malice ever spare?

Wasn't the dear St. Seraphim holy? He, too, had to endure much from evil tongues. But he, too, such a humble one, a longsuffering, true monk with sorrow, kept saying: "My joy, they rose up against lowly Seraphim, wanting to judge him: why he has done something, why I am obedient to the Mother of God." And of course as a man he also suffered from human injustice. Then there is another wondrous ascetic, the great sufferer Father Hieromonk Theophil [of Kiev]. How many sufferings he endured from the brothers! I read his life and kissed his picture. One believing priest wrote to me: "Father Gerasim, do you love the fools-for-Christ's-sake, the God-pleasers?" I was struck by this question. How can I not love, especially being a monk, the friends of God, those who pray for us sinners?! I doubt if any of the Platonite priests really venerate the saints. This is what was written in a newspaper, *Svet,* No. 32, of 1932, in an article by George Grebenshchikov, "A Path of a Hierarch," where he exclaims about his priests: "O Lord, forgive me. I am sinning by being with them.... Some of them are veritably Godless. O true God! They come to me and begin to contradict, saying: 'What kind of God is there?' O Lord! This is terrible, when a priest is an unbeliever. That means that he is not afraid of God and is fooling people."

Yes, this is frightful, when a priest does not believe in God. He is not afraid of God and is deceiving the people. And even more frightful is it that this priest tells this to his bishop, and the bishop keeps him in his diocese!!! The bishop thereby helps the atheist priest to continue deceiving the believing people who support such a parasite. O Lord, forgive us!

It is also true that the contemporary press does a lot of evil, publishing false information about the church schisms. And it is true that the bishops have begun to do something terrible. Bishop Seraphim rushes into another diocese and inflames human passions even more intensely....

From Russia sad news is sailing my way: the Bolsheviks also decided to destroy the Theophany Cathedral in Moscow. I read such a thing and could not sleep. It is our last biggest cathedral in our white-stoned Moscow. No, something frightful is coming, approaching. On Mount Athos the life of Russian monks is fading away, monks who pray for the world. A great ascetic and flaming man of prayer, Schemamonk Father Silouan, said: "Without prayer for it by holy people, the world cannot last long, troubles will begin." These troubles have already arrived!...

Lucky is Archbishop Tikhon.* The Lord has chosen him and received him in His holy abodes.... And how joyous I used to be, knowing that in the diocese of Archbishop Tikhon everything was quiet and peaceful. But the enemy and evil little people sowed dissension and made a revolution in the Church of Christ. I don't remember now which Byzantine Emperor wrote, addressing the bishops: "For me a Church division and fight is worse than terrible wars."

Yes, the little icon of the Mother of God was absolutely black, and it was difficult to discern what was engraved on it. I scrubbed it and it began to shine. Of course it is precious because it is from Holy Russia; and also because it stayed many years in Russian Alaska, on Spruce Island, where Father Herman labored and where he rests with his relics. Yes, and also this icon is so old; it is several hundred years old.

---

*Hierarch Tikhon of San Francisco, who died in March, 1962, was a disciple of St. Gabriel of Kazan, now canonized by the Kazan Diocese, 1997.

I cannot tell you what will happen on Spruce Island after my death. There will be those who will want to move there. But I see that the Leontyites are not even thinking of it, they don't care. The States were always a stepmother for poor Alaska. The Orthodox diocese of Alaska was robbed by Archbishop Platon (Rozhdestvensky) and his cunning friends. But in Russia the highest Church Authority only found out about that at the end of 1917. The report about it of the bishop of Alaska, Philip (Stavitsky), did it. But by that time the Russian Revolution had started, and a frightful time for the Orthodox Church, so that nothing could be done. Furthermore, Bishop Philip was not allowed to go abroad. Before 1909 in Alaska there was a seminary in Sitka and an orphanage. There were orphanages both in Kodiak and in Unalaska. There were many priests and schools. I still remember what we saw in Sitka in the beginning of September, 1916. We beheld the total destruction of what had been achieved with much labor by believing laymen. The grave of Elder Father Herman, who was revered by the whole of Orthodox Alaska, had also been abandoned. The chapel over his grave was built with the money of Archbishop Nicholas (Zernov), and Bishop Philip was dreaming of making at least a skete there on Spruce Island. He was a true monk and loved monasticism.

Yes, my dear one, I do not know what will be there in the hermitage on Spruce Island after my death. And I have already been here [in Alaska] for forty-five years.

You are writing to me that you have a monastic calling. It is a good thing! But you know that in such times as ours, frightful times, all Orthodox monasteries where there were wise instructors and Elder-ascetics have been destroyed. You know Father Protopresbyter Adrian (Rymarenko) who, not having a high theological education, accepted the priestly rank in the most frightful time of persecution of the Lord and His Holy Church. His wife, Matushka Eugenia Grigorievna, was an educated, wealthy woman, and they both labored in God's vineyard, enduring everything that befell them. They had children and they suffered for them. But a monk is alone, it is easier for him to labor for

Fr. Adrian Rymarenko in younger days. Later he became archbishop of New York and the founder of the New Diveyevo Monastery.

the Lord, for his holy Church and for his neighbor. Dear St. Seraphim used to love and repeat often: "No, there is nothing better than the monastic life!" And I, sinful Archimandrite Gerasim, experienced the bliss and sweetness of the monastic life while living as a novice in St. Tikhon's Monastery. Oh, how happy I used to be there; in my soul there was peace!!! Those days I shall never forget. And also I experienced unearthly joy on the day of my ordination into the rank of hierodeacon. On that day there was such joy in my soul, that I was ready to embrace the whole world, all people.

But then a terrible time struck. The Lord called our native land, our people, our mother the Orthodox Church to suffering, and now spiritual peace, joy in the Holy Spirit, rarely, very rarely, visits me. O Lord, forgive me! But even Thy great Prophet Elias, seeing the apostasy of the Israelites from God, called upon Thee: "O Lord, rather send me death, for I am no better than my fathers!" And Christ Himself sorrowed, grieved in the Garden of Gethsemane, and now there is no peace or unity in our Russian Orthodox Church.

You still are young. I think it will be easier for you to endure it. Forgive me if I am mistaken! It was a long time ago, more than thirty years, when one highly educated hierarch wrote to me: "Dear Father Gerasim! Heavy is my heart...." Yes, it was very hard for him, he was not well, and he was severely rebuked both in the press and from the church pulpit. And it was only because he remained on the side of the Synodal jurisdiction. I read his sorrowful letter, shed tears, and warmly prayed for him. His letter touched me to the depths of my soul. Although he was a bishop, a highly educated man, still after all he was human, and he was heavy-hearted, being deeply hurt. Our Archbishops would indeed make mistakes, not having compassion for the suffering of a simple monk, and so often treated them crudely. But the heart nevertheless suffers, whether that of a learned hierarch or a simple monk. And the suffering of the latter was more painful, for he often suffered alone; there was no one to defend him, to console him.

Such Archpastors as Metropolitan Philaret of Kiev, Archbishop Anthony of Voronezh, Bishop Theophan the Recluse, and other kind, true monks, were not numerous. Very many of our Elders came from the midst of simple monks, and were consolers of millions of suffering Russian people. Elder Father Herman was also from the simple monks, but he was of a kind soul, of holy life, and could freely converse with educated people. Of course he would talk about God, His love towards people, and the salvation of the soul. He was a wonderful Elder, a great ascetic!!!

It is lamentable, indeed, that our higher ecclesiastical authority in America paid no attention and did not try to collect those wonderful miracles which took place all these years, beginning in 1836 and up to today. I read somewhere that the Catholics have it easier. If there occurs one miracle at the grave of a saintly man, then they beatify him in the category of blessed ones. Bishop Alexey collected the miracles, copying everything down that the old people told him about Elder Father Herman and his miracles, including to whomever among the faithful people they occurred. But apparently, leaving America and going to the Soviet Union, he did not pass on that which he was instructed to do by his co-brothers. I also do not believe that he presented it to Patriarch Alexey in Moscow.* No, such people are thoroughly searched at the border. But now, they have forgotten all about Elder Herman and about his holy grave. They are trying to strengthen their positions in the States also. And what will happen here on Spruce Island, the Lord alone knows. Orthodoxy here is in a lamentable state. I am now old, weak, and sick. Now I am creaking like an old tree which can collapse even from a little storm. But all is in God's hands! When I am in my hermitage, I often serve the Liturgy of the holy Apostle James, the Brother of the Lord. I love its petitions, its wonderful touching prayers. They are fitting for our much-sorrowful times:

---

*This document was never officially published either during Fr. Gerasim's lifetime or afterwards.

"Remember, O Lord, all those in trouble, have mercy on all, O Master, pacify all of us, give peace to the multitude of Thy people, destroy temptations, remove wars, stop divisions in churches and the risings of the heretics do Thou speedily remove. Dispel the prejudice of the nations, uphold the Orthodox Christian nations, and Thy peace and Thy love give to us, O God our Savior, the hope of all the ends of the earth!"

Once I received newspapers, and opening them I saw at once that a fierce storm is raging in the whole world. I remember the year 1911, Mount Athos, and my reading there of the prophecies of Monk Nilus about the last years of the time of this world.* At that time these prophecies of Elder Nilus were being translated into the Russian language by Hieroschemamonk Anthony (Bulatovich). He came from a military background and knew several languages. But even then, in 1911, much was already taking place in the world about which Elder Nilus prophesied. I remember this: "And the Church of Christ will be beheaded." I read then the manuscript which Father Hieroschemamonk Anthony (Bulatovich) gave me. But after that he also left the Holy Mountain, his desert kalyve, taking the side of the Name-worshippers. Concerning this he conducted a polemical controversy in Russia with our learned theologians. And that terrible turmoil, of the Name-worshippers, was a forerunner of a great trauma for the whole Christian world. Then more than 800 monks left Athos, among whom there were many Elders and outstanding monks. That was quite a temptation!!! O Lord, forgive us!

Today is February 4th. A snowstorm! I do not feel too well; my old bones moan in such weather. I am sending my greetings to your close ones. I always pray for them. I still must write many letters, but I cannot do it right now. Alas, alas!

---

*The Orthodox Word No. 21 (Platina, California: St. Herman Brotherhood), pp. 143-149.

Yes, I had the pleasure to live in St. Tikhon's Monastery and in faraway Alaska where Father Herman met those* who also are buried in the place dear to me [St. Tikhon's Monastery]. Yes, the ways of God are unfathomable. Forgive me. Pray for me, also.

Yours truly,
A. Gerasim

LETTER 10
December 30, 1963

Dear Gleb Dimitrievich,

The mercy of God be with you!

I received from you a weighty packet in which there were a letter and a wonderful article you compiled. Yes, I lived in unforgettable St. Tikhon's Monastery more than five years. I heard about the Yanovskys while still in the monastery. Under the Transfiguration Cathedral, deep underground, there was a little church dedicated to Christ's Resurrection, where, under its vaults, many important personages were buried. I remember how expensive wreathes with black and white ribbons were preserved there. And if I am not mistaken, there was someone buried from the Yanovsky family. Unfortunately, in that beautiful little church the Lity was served only once a year on the first Sunday of Pascha. During summertime, if one of the brethren should die, then they would bury the deceased brother there. I already said that it was deep underground, and the air was always cool. The ground there is sandy and there was no moisture. The iconostasis there was of a metal mold and beautiful. Since we simple novices very rarely visited it, I did not have a chance to read the names of those slaves of God who lay there under

---

*Simeon Yanovsky (Schemamonk Sergius) and his son Hieroschemamonk Alexander (†1876). See "An Around the World Journey into Sanctity," *The Orthodox Word,* No. 150, 1990, pp. 4-109.

the gravestones of the church. But I remember well that the whole floor of the church was covered with those gravestones.

I read your collected material, and it seemed to me that I visited again that dear native corner of our Holy Russia! But remembering all that, involuntarily bitter tears poured down my face. The Vladimir Icon of the Mother of God was highly revered, and it was adorned with a riza of pearls and precious stones. It was located near the side chapel of St. Nicholas behind the left cliros. In the Transfiguration Cathedral, where the relics of St. Tikhon rested underground, there were five altars. The Cathedral was laid out with marble and richly decorated. The second Cathedral was dedicated to the Dormition. That was a splendid edifice! It was very tall, with one huge cupula, of golden refined craftsmanship. All icons were painted on zinc by the brush of an artist, but the walls were not frescoed yet. It is sad that on that place where they built a new majestic Cathedral, there originally stood an ancient wooden church dedicated to the Dormition of the Mother of God which was built during the lifetime of St. Tikhon, who served in it himself. Such precious, holy things the monks could not preserve, and our bishops as well! Even the place where St. Tikhon's Monastery was located was extremely picturesque. In the monastery there was a high, beautiful bell-tower. A bell of 1,600 poods [approximately thirty tons] was hung in August, 1906. The second bell was 600 poods [twelve tons]. In 1909, a church was blessed near the new refectory. There was also a beautiful church at the infirmary. In the monastery there were many hieromonks, but for some reason the Liturgy was served rarely in these churches. On Mount Athos in the infirmary church Liturgy was performed daily. I was able to meet many monks who knew well Archimandrite Moses.* I also knew the Kazan Convent in Kaluga.**

In his notes about Elder Herman, Yanovsky is mistaken. In the years of his stay in Kodiak, Father Herman was located in Kodiak

---

*A disciple of Elders Moses and Macarius of Optina.
** Where Yanovsky's daughter Angelina was later Abbess (†1914).

ABBESS ANGELINA
of the Kazan Mother of God Convent in Kaluga.
(1838-1914)

wherein he often visited Simeon Ivanovich Yanovsky. You visited both Kodiak and Spruce Island, and can you say that Elder Herman could have had talks with Yanovsky and then go travelling to Spruce Island!? No, he could not! This is a mistake of Elder Schemamonk Father Sergius. Father Herman lived for many long years in Kodiak. On Spruce Island he spent his last years, only thirteen years. The frightful epidemic began in Kodiak, and this is where a large barn was built for the Aleuts who belonged to the *promyshleniki.* They would gather there from all the nearby islands of Alaska. Yes, there were intervals when in Kodiak there was not a single priest. Elder Father Herman served in the church, reading the Hours and Typica. Of course he continued doing this, having moved to Spruce Island.

From the notes of those who knew him, we know that Father Herman forbade the Aleuts to inform [the authorities in Kodiak] about his death, saying to them that they should bury him themselves. He also told them how to dress him for that. The times were harsh and the Aleuts, being afraid of the authorities, decided to let those in [St. Paul's] harbor know about his death; but a storm arose, and they could not come to Spruce Island. The coffin was made in Kodiak. It was covered with black material, and inside it was lined with white. The crosses were made of golden galoon. In the book it was printed that Father Herman's relics waited for the coffin a whole month. And it turns out that Michael Zinovievich Vinokouroff (Washington, D.C.) was right in establishing that Father Herman died on Spruce Island on November 15/28, 1836. His burial took place on December 13/26. And all these years, starting from 1935, I have been celebrating the day of his repose on [November] 15/28. His nameday is on the 28th of June, old style.

The old lady Alexandra Charalampievna Ilarionova [Wotch] used to tell me the following, which took place during the last years of his life: "Mother used to relate that when Father Herman would arrive in Kodiak, then everyone would hurry to greet him, and everywhere could be heard: 'Appa has arrived, Appa has arrived!' Even the old lady

Alexandra Ivanovna Wotch received from him healing from a frightful migraine headache.

A new calamity has struck Spruce Island Hermitage. There they are cutting down trees, and a tractor is rumbling. I do not know how much land belongs to the Russian Orthodox mission. Our times are frightful! All the powers of hell have arisen against Orthodoxy! And involuntarily one asks the Lord: "O Lord, why is the path of the iniquitous so rapidly widening?!!"

I spent from May 29 to September 15 in my desert hermitage. My health is bad, and I am often tired out. After all, I'm now seventy-five years old. My sight grows weak, and life becomes more sorrowful. The Aleuts and Creoles are drinking, carousing. It is hard here, too, to work in the vineyard of Christ.

I shudder up to today when I think of how an Orthodox Christian could deposit you with suitcases in the Lagoon—a man who for the first time had arrived in Alaska, not knowing that this is only the grave of the Elder—and throw him on the shore, leaving him all alone. I don't know what kind of heart he had!! And it's questionable whether he has one. And Michael Chernikoff, whom you asked: "How can I get to Fr. Gerasim?" said to someone: "I thought that this was some kind of a swindler." Now he has become rich and he becomes proud. That uncouth Aleut!

On the 28th of December, by evening I received my mail. The Russian newspapers contain frightful news. They disturbed me to such an extent that I could not sleep the whole night. My soul pains for the Orthodox Church! And, of course, on the 29th I barely could serve Liturgy. At four in the afternoon I served a moleben to the Mother of God and read an akathist to the Reigning [Icon of the] Mother of God. And the whole day I was nervous. One wants to cry and weep! I cannot give advice to an educated hierarch, but I think, why does Archbishop John not forbid his fans to praise him as a saint and a miracle-worker? After all, this is a monastic counsel, an order: "Do not deify anyone during his lifetime." All our ascetics were afraid of that, as of the fire of

Gehenna. O Lord, forgive us! And now the conflict has hit the whole diocese in California! The Lord doesn't hear the prayers of sinful Monk Gerasim. Oh, how I grieve that I cannot seclude myself in my beloved desert hermitage, and there in the quietude of my cell call upon the Lord in this frightful time: "Oh, give peace, O Lord, to the church divisions!!!" I'm praying also to St. Seraphim and to Blessed Elder Theophil.

Today after Liturgy I gave a sermon in English. I said to the people: "I am no saint, but I will be happy if the Lord will call me to Himself." The people are demoralized, they do not listen. You saw how Aleuts came to Spruce Island for the feast day of the Dormition of the Mother of God and were not in church, but were smoking.

Last summer the weather was bad, and on the 14th and 18th [of August] no one could come to me. But I served all by myself and was ecstatic. The ascetics say that the house of God during church services is never empty, and I, not even being healthy, nevertheless managed to serve the complete service, not omitting anything. And of course, I thought about you there, but, O my God! How difficult to bear this church division, this sinful squabble!!! Besides, my health is poor, my legs torture me, and everything.

In Russia my sister Eugenia died on the 16th of March, 1963. The funeral was conducted in the church in our own Dormition Cathedral. Indeed, it is the only one that is open. And another thing that upset my soul was the writing of a Catholic priest who spent long years in Siberia.

I did not notice, right away, the end of your letter. Yes, such a thing is very sad. Man throws himself on all sides, changes religion like a gypsy changes horses. Pray to Blessed Elder Theophil. Ask from him advice and help. But I feel sorry for your sister. Reading your letter, the end of it, I at once thought of Elder Hieroschemamonk Theophil, of his wise advice to those who ask of him, and of his venerators. These God-pleasers hear us from the other world.

Well, was I happy today that I found an icon for you of the Mother of God, and what kind of an icon! A very ancient one, the Mother of

Father Gerasim's sister Eugenia, who kept in contact with her brother for many years, shown here with her husband Stephen in the early 1930's.

God "Joy of All Who Sorrow." All this time I have thought of how I could get for you something dearly Russian, old and ancient. I do not know when it came to Alaska. One thing I know, that in Russia such icons were cast 250-300 years ago. In Russia I left triptychs of twelve major feast days. Oh, how I regret that I did. They were ancient and saturated with prayer. Yesterday I received your address from Fr. Vladimir from the monastery. See, I think of you. I planned to write to you for quite some time.

If you read the new newspaper *New Dawn,* then of course you know that there was a fire in Ouzinkie at the beginning of May.* In this fire two children died. On July 12th their grandmother died. In August her granddaughter, who was brought up by Baptists, shot herself. The whole summer was not a joyful one for me. In Kodiak is the learned priest Makary Targansky; I have nothing in common with him. He does not serve All-night Vigils, except for serving a funeral for Gene Sundberg's Aunt Tatiana.

I'm writing a long letter to Bishop Ambrose. I wrote to him in spring, also; no answer followed. Oh, how difficult it is to work in the vineyard of God.

Today is the 30th of December. It is quiet and dry. No rain. I slept better. But I took a sleeping pill. The church fight in California gives me no rest. And although I know that Archbishop Tikhon is no longer, that he is there where there is no longer sighing, nor sickness, nor earthly sorrow, nevertheless, I feel sorry for this good, faithful hierarch-monk! Do you know that they say that angels weep also?

The article of your writing on Elder Herman and his friends is wonderful. But I think that it is time for us to correct something: what Simeon Ivanovich Yanovsky (in schema Sergius) wrote which was not correct. In the days when Yanovksy lived in Kodiak at the same time that Elder Father Herman was in Kodiak, after conversations which often lasted way beyond midnight, the Elder could not go to Spruce

---

*The house of Emil Anderson burned down on May 5, 1963.

Island, which is separated [from Kodiak] by a boisterous strait. The East Cape is also very dangerous, where there are rocks which rarely leave it without danger. On that place, even during my stay in Alaska, many schooners, boats, and motor boats with people perished. I know this place. I myself almost perished there. And Elder Father Herman could not have rowed to Spruce Island in a leather baidarka, which is a little skin boat. It is also unknown whether he could make his voyages in it. Afognak Island is located twenty-eight miles from Kodiak, but the Elder was not there during all the long years of his stay in Kodiak. On Afognak Island there were three settlements: Big Afognak, Katani, and Little Afognak. Now I don't recall how many years Father Herman lived on Spruce Island; it is either fifteen or sixteen years. In Ouzinkie he had nothing. It is not true, which many have written, that S. I. Yanovsky was there where our mission was and that Valaam monks lived there. I do not know where the first church was located, nor the semblance of a monastery next to it. There was a persecution of Fr. Herman; many slandered him very much. He ran away to Spruce Island from the evil tongues of people. Baranov was a crude, unmannered man, and he was not a lover of monasticism.

Well, I received mail again. I read *New Dawn:* a letter of Archbishop Seraphim Ivanov, and again my nerves began to moan. I do not know who could love our Mother the Orthodox Church and not be forced to suffer, reading the outrage that is going on in California. Here my Aleuts do not understand; it cannot touch them. And I do not call them to pray, as used to be done in Holy Russia before the thrice-cursed Revolution.

I love my desert Hermitage, my quiet nook. But now, being seventy-five years old and not having good health, "then prepare yourself for tribulation." Hard times have arrived; there is no peace on the earth. Even in Vancouver, in the Leontyite parish, things go badly. There are mostly parishioners from the intelligentsia.

Alexandra Chichenova, Mrs. Alice Kreuger, died in Seattle, Washington last summer. She would often send oil for the lampada that burns at Elder Herman's. And if I find myself in Ouzinkie, it is still burning here with me.

Thank you for the little icons of Elder Fr. Herman. I always remember in prayer your close ones: the handmaiden of God Nina, Ia, and those whom you wrote down on a list. I think that Father Abbot Ambrose is already back in the Monastery. He is already an elder, he is eighty years old. Batiushka Father Vladimir always answers my letters like a Christian, like a good monk. Gene [Sundberg] I have not seen since August. They, too, rarely write. He works and is very busy. Fr. Makary Targansky returned to Kodiak on the 17th of September. Orthodoxy in Alaska is dying. Young priests do not want to go to Alaska. But God knows best.

Thank you for the letter and article. May God reward you.

Your
Archimandrite Gerasim

P.S. After all, Spruce Island is not as they have drawn it. On it there is a tall, beautiful mountain. And in circumference it is more than 52 miles. That which they have drawn looks more like that little island which is located on the western side. At low tide I walked there more than once. Spruce Island is rather big, with a big mountain, and from the eastern side it is beautiful.

In 1934, the end of August, at the time when the Platonites maliciously armed themselves against me and strove to prevent me from going to Spruce Island, I saw a dream: I was in Afognak. It was as if I were walking somewhere near a tall mountain. The place was beautiful. Around me were growing spruces, there was green grass. I heard bell-ringing, and I thought to myself, "There is probably a monastery here, let me go and see." I walked and saw that between some young little spruces there stood a monk of not large stature, who kindly said to me: "It is I who am ringing here the Paschal bells." And he consoled me, telling me who was against me. I woke up and joy visited my soul, and I said: "Father Herman is on my side. I am not afraid of anyone!" And on the 26th of August, 1935, I moved to Spruce Island. That was

A view from Monks' Lagoon facing the ocean: a little islet which is accessible from the shore at low tide. In St. Herman's time it may have been a garden area. This resembles the drawing of Yanovsky.

the nameday of my mother Natalia. And in 1914 on the 26th of August, I left my native Tula forever.

A. G.

LETTER 11
March 16, 1964

Deeply respected Gleb Dimitrievich,

I am greeting you and your close ones with the soul-saving Great Lent. I received your card. But forgive me, I cannot fulfill your request. I do not have any earth here [in Ouzinkie] from the grave of Elder Father Herman. And I do not know if anyone among the inhabitants of Ouzinkie has it. The weather here is very stormy, and since March first is very cold. Everyone is at work, and no one has visited my hermitage. I read your article on Elder Herman in the newspaper *Russian Life.* Concerning the letter of Archpriest A. Popov telling you that he allegedly was informed about more than a hundred miracles of Elder Father Herman, I beg you not to believe such a lying canonist and false doctor of theology. Alexander Popov served in Kodiak for five years and for all those years he pocketed for himself all those dollars which the citizens of the Kodiak parish gave him for candles and oil for the chapel [at Monks' Lagoon]. Now is that a priest that believes in God?! Do not think that this is slander against him. The last year of his stay in Alaska, when I was in Kodiak, a man from the Three Hierarchs Village of Old Harbor, Alexis D., visited me and asked: "Father Gerasim, our inhabitants asked me, if you are in Kodiak, to visit you and to ask you whether you received those dollars which we donated for Father Herman?" I answered: "No, not a single penny." He then sadly answered: "We knew it. That means everything went into his priest's pockets!" And also Fr. Archpriest Gregory Glebov, having lived in Kodiak for seven years, did not give me a cent of what people had donated for the Spruce Island Hermitage. I wrote about that to Bishop John [Zlobin] and to the Metropolia. But they are "their own people," and they defend "their own." If it were the truth that A. Popov heard from people more than a hundred miracles of Elder Father Herman, then they would be known to me also. Well, at least half of them. After all, I have now been living in these places since February, 1917.

Let me say something else: since 1917 I have served pannikhidas on the nameday of Elder Father Herman, on the 28th of June, old style, and talked about him to my congregation.

When I was the head of the parish in Afognak, Alaska, for eighteen whole years, on Great Friday, decorating the coffin for Christ's burial shroud, I would place on the western side an icon of the Mother of God, "Weep Not For Me, O Mother." The icon was large, on paper, but a good print. And when the shroud was taken out and placed upon the table-coffin, then a row of candles would be lit near the coffin of Christ, right before the icon of the Mother of God, "Weep Not For Me, O Mother." This whole scene was touching, unto tears! A picture presented itself that reminded one of that terrible scene on Golgotha on Good Friday. It is impossible to convey with a pen that which the believing soul of a human being experiences.

And absolutely everybody loved it. One Orthodox family, the Martinsens, moved from Afognak to Seward, Alaska, where they had lived for several years. But when an air base was built in Kodiak and there were many jobs available, they all moved to Kodiak. The wife of John Martinsen often remembered her native place, Afognak, and the church service I celebrated there. Each time she would remember the Good Friday service and the icon of the Mother of God, "Weep Not For Me, O Mother," and would say:

"Father Gerasim, if I ever should get some money, then I would ask you to order such an icon for me. This is my long-time wish, my promise." So I ordered such a one from Mount Athos, both because Mount Athos is the earthly lot of the Queen of Heaven, and also because the monks there are experiencing poverty—to give them a few

Afognak during Great Friday, with the icon "Weep Not for Me,
O Mother," arranged by Fr. Gerasim as he saw it in Russia.

dollars for a piece of bread. The icon was large, on canvas, and was wonderfully painted. On it the Mother of God, the "Sorrowful Mother," is painted alone. Just as I asked the monks to paint, the robes of the Mother of God are deep blue, and out of Her eyes tears stream down. I was there in Kodiak when the icon arrived. I opened it up in the presence of eleven other people. Since the fishing season had just opened, the Martinsens brought the icon to Priest A. Popov and told him: "In the fall after the work of fishing is through, we will order a frame and a stand for it." I had already overheard that A. Popov said to someone: "I have in New York good painters who for the same money ($25.00) could paint a much better one." In the autumn of the same year I chanced to be in Kodiak and visited the church. What I saw then shocked me and painfully outraged me!!! On the icon I saw a thick black grating, as is done before beginning to make a copy. And the priest A. Popov said to me: "Evidently that icon was painted by one who was still a beginner. I tried to wash off these black lines, but couldn't." What could I say to such an outrageous liar, such a Godless man?!! That very day I was standing in church before that icon of the Mother of God and from heart-felt sorrow I could not open my eyes during the whole liturgy. I wrote about all that in detail to Archimandrite Vladimir, the abbot of the Cell of St. Nicholas "Burazeri" on Mount Athos.... But when A. Popov left for the States and I came to church, then the lines were no longer there.

Today is Forgiveness Sunday. All day we have had a snowstorm, and it is cold. At night I slept only three hours, and all day today I have felt sad.... Forgive me that I still cannot send to you earth from Elder Herman's grave. Yes, I smelled an unearthly fragrance on the spot of the blessed repose of Elder Herman on the 14th/27th of May in 1927. I will never forget that day! The weather was wonderful, the sun shone brightly, the birds sang cheerfully. I went down on my knees and said: "Father Herman, Christ is Risen!" And at that moment I was surrounded by such a fragrance as I have never smelled before! No, it was not a fragrance of aromatic incense, it was a paradisal fragrance, the soul of the Elder visited his beloved hermitage! I believe so! And in 1935 my persecution began, not on the part of the Godless Bolsheviks, but from the Platonites. Much have I endured in these years here. I am now an old man, more than seventy-five years of age, and my health is bad. But God knows best! I beg God that I would be able to die here.

I read your article, "Father Herman, Miracle-worker of America" once more. No, it is not true what the "canonist" A. Popov wrote to you! Bishop Alexey visited all the parishes of the Alaskan diocese and, of course, conducted talks everywhere about Elder Herman. This Popov stayed only in the Kodiak parish with its little adjacent villages. During his stay in Alaska all the old people had already died, who in their days had heard much about Elder Herman and his help from the life beyond the grave. And besides, A. Popov is a master in inventing that which never took place.

Here let me tell you something that is not religious. While still in Afognak I read the first part of a novel, *Two Brothers*. For more than thirty years I had been looking for the second part. I wrote to numerous people in the States who had many Russian books and promised to return the book at once by registered mail, but no one answered me. The Popovs told me more than once that they had read through all the Russian classics of our literature. So I told him much of the content of the novel *Two Brothers*. I told him: "I would like to know what happened at the conclusion and whom Kolya married." At the end of Part I it was said that the well-educated, intelligent Nicholas began to court the shy girl Helen, who was already preparing to be the wife of that kind, honest landowner, who loved her. But a beautiful girl Nina played a large part in the story; she was not a serious woman, but like a beautiful tiger. I told all that to Popov, and said: "Judging from the novel, at the end of it Nicholas most likely will marry Helen." Then A. Popov self-assuredly answered: "I read this novel. I remember everything, and I tell you that Nicholas marries the beautiful Nina...." But judging from how Nicholas' and Basil's parents viewed Nina and their general home life, it was hard to believe that such a thing would happen. Besides, the father of Nicholas was a "holy" man. He used to say to his beloved son Nicholas: "Kolya, I do not like to talk about people, but I will tell you—be careful with Nina, people say many negative things about her!!"

Later, when [Fr. Roman] Stürmer had lived in Kodiak for three or four years, I received from Washington the book *Two Brothers*. Both volumes were bound into one book. Having received the book, I lay down in bed and began to read the book from the beginning (both volumes).

Do not laugh at a monk, that he loves to read novels. But I wanted to know whether our learned priest, our priest-canonist, our priest doctor of theology, had told me the truth. I, not closing my eyes, read the whole night, and of course A. Popov had told a lie! It turned out that neither he nor his wife had read that novel; he only knew of it what I had told him. This is how dangerous it is to believe even a priest in our evil times. But I see that such ones are held in respect in our Platonite Metropolia.

Father Anatole Blessed the Big Chapel

Today is the 3rd/16th of March. Everywhere there are heaps of snow and a cruel northerly wind. Indeed like [in A. S. Pushkin's poem]:

> Blizzard clouds roll in, foreboding,
> Blowing snow-gusts on their flight,
> Like wild beasts they howl, bemoaning,
> Or like infants cry at night.

I worry about my hermitage, my chapels, and my little house. Everything there is surrounded by tall old trees. Last year, 1963, was also a stormy winter, and many trees fell. Two trees fell not far from my chapel and closed the path to it. But for these long years, from the day my chapel was built during the episcopacy of Bishop Nicholas Zernov, not a single tree had fallen near the chapel.

The chapel was blessed by Archimandrite Anatole Kamensky. In 1911-12 he was a vicar bishop to Archbishop Dimitry of Cherson and

St. Andrew the Apostle Church in Kalisnoo,
which Fr. Gerasim visited while in Sitka.

New Martyr Bishop
Anatole (Kamensky)

Young Fr. Gerasim,
photographed in Sitka.

Odessa. In 1916, in November, I chanced to visit Kilisnoo Island, located not far from Sitka. At the time a fair-sized chapel dedicated to the Holy Apostle Andrew the First-called stood there, and there was a large-sized icon covered with a gilded riza of beautiful workmanship. The chapel was located high on a hill, and the view of the sea from there was wonderful. Nearby was a little house with four rooms. In that house lived the church warden Charalampus Sokolov and his wife Mary. There Sokolov showed me a letter from Bishop Anatole, sent to him from Odessa, Russia. This is how the learned Bishop Anatole complained to his former worker who labored in the Orthodox Alaska vineyard:

"Dear Charalampus," wrote Bishop Anatole, "pray to God that the Holy Synod would give me a diocese. Then I will call you to come with your lady to Russia where we will spend the rest of our lives. My ruling Archbishop, Dimitry, is an angry old man. To live with such a one is as difficult as for a church psalmist with an angry priest."

Yes, such things did happen in Holy Russia that, like the Cherson hierarch, they would always blame their lesser co-brothers and make them suffer. Such a thing is clearly apparent from the biography of the Kievan Metropolitan Philaret [Amphiteatrov, †1857], who was like a mother to all monks! This is what he wrote to his brother-bishops who would write bad things about those whom this kindest bishop would receive in the Lavra [Kiev Caves] or in other monasteries in the Kievan diocese:

"Please don't write to me unkind things about those monks who have come to the Lavra. They are all good, kind monks, but they left their monasteries because of the unkindness of their abbots...." Yes, such things took place.

Shcheglovsk Monastery

At a distance of three miles from Tula there was a well-off men's monastery dedicated to the Nativity of the Theotokos. In that monastery there labored and struggled a certain hieromonk, Father Innocent.

He was a kind man, a humble monk. One day he was appointed to be abbot in a smaller monastery in the same diocese. Father Innocent was a man of weak temperament, but he was kind. He did like to drink a glass or two, though. And knowing his own weakness, he declined such a high position. But they did not listen to him, appointing him anyway, "as an obedience," as it was customary to say. In the new place he began to drink a lot more. And the monks and novices, noticing his weakness and kindness, began to offer him more. Of course the ruling bishop found out about it and he was expelled. So he wanted to return to his old monastery where he had given his monastic vows. But by that time a new abbot had been appointed, a learned bishop, a doctor of theology—Bishop Evdokim Meshchersky, who did not accept him into this Shcheglovsk Monastery. And so the poor elder Abbot Innocent had to seek shelter for himself in a different diocese, that of Kaluga, while Bishop Evdokim himself liked to drink vodka. Is it not true that we suffer for our own self-love?!

Miracle of Saint Seraphim of Sarov

Yesterday was the first day of Great Lent. The storm is cruel, and it lasted for the whole day. In my apartment it is very cold.

Today I read the heart-rending canon of St. Andrew, bishop of Crete. I read it in my cell. People are working in the cannery. Besides, when it is so cold it is impossible to serve in such a cold church! I simply love this heart-rending canon!!!

You are doing a good deed, organizing a Brotherhood in the name of St. Herman, Wonderworker of Alaska. May God help you! But remember that satan does not like it; he does his evil to those who glorify the chosen ones of God. I experienced this myself, when I came to Alaska and began to glorify St. Seraphim of Sarov.

When I lived in Afognak, Alaska, there was a creole, Theodotus Grigoriev, who had a hernia. At one time he lifted his boat and suffered a "strangulation" of the hernia. I was summoned to him, and he was lying there suffering. From the doctor's "self-help" book I found out that if the hernia would not go back into its place (now I don't remember in what period of time), then the man dies in terrible pain. He had a wife, a large family, a crowd of children, and an old mother, a kind old grandma. I knew well that St. Seraphim loved children, and I began to pray to him that he would have mercy on the man because of his children. And what do you know! I heard that his hernia quickly went back inside to its place. The next day when I came to visit him, he began to thank me, but I said to him: "Do not thank me, but thank St. Seraphim of Sarov. I merely asked his help. I'll come again and we shall serve a thanksgiving moleben [service]." Before that, this Theodotus used to drink occasionally, but after he got well he became sober. Now he is no longer alive. He died like a Christian. Yes, wondrous is God in His saints, the God of Israel!!!

I am sending my offering for the needs of the Brotherhood in the name of Elder Herman. I am also sending my greetings to all. May Christ protect you, and His pure Mother!

Yours in spirit,
A. Gerasim

The storm rages mercilessly. I think of the birds, they must be cold.

P.S. Today is March 5/18. A freezing day. Yesterday, March 4th, was my nameday [St. Gerasim of the Jordan]. I spent it alone in my cell. I read a book, *Seer of the Future,* a work of Priest Alexander Kolesnikov. It is a wonderful book!!! If only I had a congregation that knew Russian, then I would have done what in former Tsarist Russia took place in many parishes: wherever there was a parish school, I would give spiritual public talks. I would read this book aloud. But alas! My parishioners do not know the Russian language, neither do they know English well enough! It is amazing, they sit in school for eight years and cannot read well. And we "outdated" Russians, having completed primary school in three years, are already able to read all books, all our classics, as well as spiritual books, lives of saints, etc!

Here in the village it is hard to walk. Everything is covered with ice, and I cannot go and ask the older parishioners whether they have some earth from Elder Herman's grave. Oh, how sad it is for a monk during the days of Great Lent!!! How I wish I were on the Holy Mountain of Athos during these days. Oh, my Athos, my priceless Athos. Father Hieroschemamonk Nikon Shrantmer visited me for a month on Afognak. But he did not write to me, although I helped him quite a bit! But one must pray for all, while we are still alive. Forgive me.

A. G.

LETTER 12
March 6/19, 1964

Dear Brother Gleb,

Yesterday, 5/18, I sent you a registered letter, and today, 6/19, I received a letter from Athos, Greece. This is what Elder Father Ignatius writes to me, who is the abbot of the Cell of St. Ignatius the God-Receiver: "Here on Mount Athos we have many changes. They have constructed roads for buses and airstrips. The Greeks are triumphant about it; they're building, repairing. And the Russians are dying out. In the Monastery of the Great Martyr Panteleimon there are forty men. And they are all feeble, blind, lame, or paralyzed. In St. Andrew's Skete—five men. In St. Elias' Skete—five men. In my skete I am alone. In the Skete of St. Chrysostom—one man. In the Skete of the Holy Trinity—one man—and he is sick. And so on, and so on. We are dying off, the last Russian monks!"

I read that, and my soul began to moan. Alas! My priceless Mount Athos has lost its desert beauty of virginity. I cry and I weep! In the night on the eve of Sunday, from the 14th to the 15th, I could not sleep; my soul was sorrowful, and I prayed and thought: something sorrowful awaits me too? Athos, that holy mountain, has been known to me from early childhood. My aunt [Angelina] lived in Moscow, where both she and her aunt, a rich woman, used to be visited by Father Archimandrite

Gabriel and his monks.* They would give them gifts of icons and books and would tell much about the Holy Mountain. Hearing all this, I was burning with a desire to visit Holy Athos, its monasteries, its sketes and cells. O, my God! How hard it is to hear such things about the Holy Mountain!!! After all, I saw all its beauty when there were many monks and wondrous church services! In the Monastery of the Great Martyr Panteleimon there were more than 2,000 monks, and divine services! In St. Andrew's Skete, more than 500. In the Skete of Holy Prophet Elias, about 400. And in our so-called cell dwellings (kalyves) there were as many as eighty, seventy, sixty, fifty, forty, and even less. On the patronal feasts, hundreds of monks would gather together and serve solemnly. And now what!?! They have turned even this Holy Place, a wondrous place, into some sort of resort. It is sad, I grieve very much!!! Father Ignatius writes:! "The Greeks are triumphant." What is there to be triumphant about?!! One should weep and lament, pray to God, to the Mother of God.

I visited Athos in the beginning of October, 1911. I remember everything, absolutely everything, that I saw there with my own eyes. I remember that foggy morning when we walked to St. Andrew's Skete. During that autumn month, Mount Athos was green, which usually occurs in the spring in the north. O, how beautiful St. Andrew's Skete was then!! It was literally a wonderful lavra! There was a grandiose cathedral, the largest in the whole of the Holy Mountain, and still sixteen churches more. Two of them, dedicated to the Mother of God and St. Innocent, were also large and beautiful. And the little ones which I loved to visit were so wonderful. But now, when I remember that there are airplanes and all contemporary devil's-works, then my soul moans. Of course, all that is allowed by God for people's sins! How

---

*Now St. Gabriel is a canonized saint. His relics lie incorrupt in Odessa in the St. Elias Mt. Athos metochion-podvorye. He was Abbot of St. Elias' Skete on Mt. Athos, which was founded by St. Paisius Velichkovsky, and he continued St. Paisius' tradition up to recent times. During all the years since he visited Mt. Athos, Fr. Gerasim corresponded with the abbots of that Russian skete, leaving several letters to them.

ST. GABRIEL OF MT. ATHOS,
Archimandrite of St. Elias Skete on Mount Athos.
He built a metochion of St. Elias Skete in Odessa, where he died
in 1901 and where he has recently begun to work miracles.
His relics were discovered, and he was canonized two years ago.

tidy Athonite monks are: the letter was written on Russian stationery from October 29, 1911. The main censor was Archimandrite Alexander. And this is that very year when I visited Mount Athos.

This very censor, Father Archimandrite Alexander, after the Russian Revolution, occupied a diocese in Poland in the rank of Bishop, and then Archbishop.

Today is the 19th and the sun is shining, but it is cold. According to the calendar it is already spring. From early childhood years, as soon as it was the first of March I would say: "Mother, today is the first of March, spring has arrived!" And this has remained with me. But in Russia, from the fourth of March (old style) robins would fly, and they would cry aloud. This would announce the arrival of spring. In Russia, in my part of it, it was a noisy time, a joyous one. Our wise peasants well remarked about that. For March 9/22 [the feast of the Forty Martyrs of Sebaste] they would bake skylarks [cookies in the shape of skylarks], and under the vault of the deep azure sky, hundreds of them would sing their wonderful songs, those pretty birds, skylarks. Oh, how we all loved that. I would run to school and see that all my school-chums had brought these fragrant, flushed swallow-cakes. Oh, how we all loved them. That dear, unforgettable childhood.

Well enough, well, I'll burst into tears. Forgive me for this sad epistle. The letter from Athos disturbed me so. It made me nervous, but who is not nervous in our terrible times?!

I am sending my greetings to your close ones. May God protect you.

Yours truly,

the sorrowful A. Gerasim

P.S. Perhaps you already read the life and great deeds of Hierarch Innocent of Irkutsk, published by the convent in the city of San Francisco. One reads such things as this, and thinks: "What heroes there used to be in previous years. How many sorrows they endured!" And that was when Sibera was still wild and where it was difficult to travel. But there were evil and proud people even there, as is evident from the books in Kodiak in the old church which burned, where his

Изображеніе съ подлинной иконы
Св. ИННОКЕНТІЙ, Епископа Иркутскаго, чудотворца.

ST. INNOCENT OF IRKUTSK,
protector for Far Eastern Siberia and America.

beautiful icon used to be. It was painted on canvas, and on it the hierarch was painted in full stature. There was a side-altar on the left dedicated to St. Innocent. At one time, I served there on the day of his commemoration. There was also an icon of analogion size, which had been blessed on the relics of the hierarch. All that perished in the fire. Of course, one should not write about that, but I think that the Lord allowed that for the sins of the son of Fr. Sisinius King. His son got mixed up with a girl of light-minded caliber, and they made themselves a bed in the church and sinned there. They found out from the blankets and other things that it belonged to the Kings. I do not know if the Platonites and their bishops know about it. But all people in Kodiak knew about it. Yes, many ancient valuable church vessels perished there, including three silver chalices. They had all been gilded. I heard that this ancient Russian secret was forgotten in later years in Russia. There were three large, wonderful altar Gospels and one small one, and a beautiful tabernacle of rare craftsmanship. But concerning the vestry, there was nothing rare. Perhaps the priests sold them, cutting them into pieces. Such things did take place here. When I came to Kodiak in 1917, at the end of January I visited that church. Oh, how it reminded me of Russia and its wooden churches. I served in it in July, 1917, on the day of the Kazan Icon of the Mother of God. I co-served with Bishop Philip Stavitsky. He died in Moscow and was buried in Astrakhan. He was a good hierarch from Volhynia, a disciple and venerator of Metropolitan Anthony of Volhynia.

And if Bishop Philip were in Alaska, then something would have been created on Spruce Island. He was a monk and a lover of monks. He went to Russia for the Council at the end of 1917. He wanted to proclaim the whole truth about the diocese of Alaska, in what a pitiful state he saw it. He also worked for the Alaskan diocese to be separated from the United States, to make it an independent diocese. He wrote that Patriarch Tikhon as well as many of the members of the council were in agreement with it. But in those days it was difficult to do anything about ecclesiastical matters, because in Russia a severe uproar was erupting, a storm of human passions. This bishop could not leave the border to go abroad. He was appointed to Smolensk. From Smolensk he was sent to Solovki for ten years as a prisoner. I do not know, I did not hear, when he returned. In the Journal of the Moscow Patriarchate I saw his picture. His shaven beard (imprisoned clergy were shorn) was again growing and was half grey. His panagia and pectoral cross have been preserved. When Patriarch Alexey was elected, Bishop Philip was one of the oldest hierarchs of the Russian Church. He delivered a wonderful homily then. But here in America he was slandered. He was not against the Patriarchate or involved in any heresies. He did not get married, as one Archimandrite wrote to me. Neither was Archbishop Evdokim married. How could he, he was already an old, sick man. But it is true that he, Hierarch Evdokim, was emotionally sick and was in a sanatorium in Sochi in the Crimea. He returned to Moscow in October, 1938, and he died there on the 22nd of October of the same year. About his death and burial almost nobody knew anything. The believing Orthodox Russian people could not forgive him that he had raised the question of closing all monasteries in Holy Russia. A group of Russians meeting him on the streets of Moscow told him this straight out. It is sad!!!

But in Tula I remember how beautifully he spoke in defense of monasteries and monks. To one novice, who was dreaming of getting married because of his family situation, he gently, sorrowfully, said: "My dear one, one cannot cheat the soul." That man's fate was decided—he did not get married.

Well, forgive me.

Your
A. Gerasim

LETTER 13
December 17, 1964

Dear Gleb Dimitrievich,

The mercy of God be with you!

Forgive me for a long silence. I left my Hermitage on the 23rd of September, of course, as each time, with pain of heart. Even that terrible earthquake did not straighten us out, did not bring us to repentance. And that not only in Alaska, but in the whole world as well. It is sad!

I am already an old man, and it is indeed time for me to seclude myself in a monastic cell.

I ordered the book on Elder Schema-archimandrite Gabriel* by mail and already have read it several times. Forgive me, but I cannot understand how Father Gabriel could decide to leave Optina Monastery, such a "spiritual hospital" of the Russian people?! And besides, having lived in it for five years, to run to the noisy city of Moscow. In connection with this I remember how Bishop Theophan the Recluse wrote to some hieromonk, who was intending to visit Moscow: "Moscow hits hard" [a Russian pun]. It is apparent here that the holy righteous recluse did not particularly wish that a monk linger in our noisy capital.

Furthermore, the fragrant aroma in the cell of Fr. Gabriel was mentioned in the book as being similar to perfume, which is invented by people. The paradisal aroma, however, as sensed by many of our holy people (ascetics) is in no way reminiscent of perfume, even the most expensive ones.

In 1926, on the 14/27 of May, when I visited the desert hermitage of Elder Fr. Herman, praying on the spot of his blessed repose where a little chapel has now been built, and when I exclaimed, "Christ is Risen,

---

One of the Ancients, available in English translation from St. Herman Press, Platina, 1988.

ST. GABRIEL OF PSKOV AND KAZAN,
canonized recently by the Kazan Diocese, where he works miracles.

Batiushka Fr. Herman!" I was surrounded by a strong aroma. It was similar to fragrant incense from Mount Athos, but in no way to those perfumes which are sold all over the world. This was the second time such a thing occurred to me in my life.

In St. Tikhon's Monastery, at the end of January, 1907, Hierodeacon Jerome reposed. He had a chronic epileptic sickness with seizures. One evening he went to light a lamp in the corridor with a wax candle stub. In the corridor of the infirmary (where he worked) he fell down and his hair caught fire, as well as his rather solid beard. The candle was burning on his chest, and his cassock and under garments were burned.

Since there wasn't anyone ill upstairs [in the infirmary], I had gone to the icon-making shop, where we mounted paper icons on boards and covered them with glass and tin frames. I came to the infirmary around 5:00 in the evening. I came into the corridor, and a terrible smell of burnt wool hit me. I quickly opened my cell, lit the lamp, and saw that a man entered my room who had the voice of Fr. Jerome, but without beard or hair. It was a frightful sight!!! That was in December of 1906. He lay sick about a month, and then Father Schema Hierodeacon Jerome died. He was tonsured into the schema before that. He had a blessed repose. Dying, he parted with me, saying that he promised to pray for me, if the Lord would vouchsafe him blessedness in the afterlife. In June of 1907 I saw a dream, that I was walking toward our Transfiguration Cathedral, and I saw that Father Schema-Hierodeacon Jerome was standing near his grave in mantle and klobuk. And he looked young, about thirty years old. Everything he was wearing was new. The same evening at about five o'clock as I came up to the door of my cell I was surrounded by a wonderful fragrance, as if someone had just censed with sweet Athonite incense. I checked all the cells, and they all were locked. The elders then were in church, and the infirmarian Fr. Myron was downstairs in the pharmacy. I then told that to my Elder Schemamonk Father Ioasaph. Hearing me out, he answered: "Misha, you told me that Father Jerome promised you to pray for you if the Lord would vouchsafe him a blessed afterlife. And now, if you would not have been afraid, he would have appeared to you in reality, as such a thing does happen and did. But you were nervous, and he could not appear to you. But his soul visited you, for this fragrance gave you to understand that he is enjoying blessedness in the heavenly abodes and is praying for you."

But that fragrance which I smelled there near the door of my cell was impossible to compare with any perfumes, even if very expensive. This is what I cannot understand from the life of Elder Father Gabriel. It is true, though, that in our monasteries the monastic tonsure was considered as some sort of distinction, as an award; and the abbots often avoided tonsuring those ryassaphore novices they did not like. But monks who knew Holy Scripture, lives of saints, or monks who loved their monastery, would endure everything patiently.

In Kaluga in the archbishop's residence there lived and struggled a certain hierodeacon, a wonderful prosphora baker. The bishop of Kaluga was a certain Benjamin [Muratovsky], a former priest-widower from Kazan. He was an imposing figure, served beautifully, and read very expressively. He carried himself with self-importance. He did not converse with monks. There was always some young lady with him, an aunt? During the summertime the bishop resided in the Monastery of St. Lawrence, which is located not too far from the city. That location was just beautiful, with wonderful fresh air. That "aunt," however, also moved into the monastery hotel, occupying the better apartments. Of course, everyone gossiped that she was the archbishop's love-interest.

Once this hierodeacon-prosphora baker handed in a request to his bishop, requesting to go to another poorer, newly organized monastery of St. Sergius of Radonezh, which was located at a distance of six miles from St. Tikhon's Monastery. Both the builder and abbot of that monastery was a monk of holy life, then still a hieromonk, Gerasim. But that hierodeacon never told anyone why he left that good position at the bishop's residence and went to the poorest of monasteries. Father Gerasim petitioned for his ordination to hieromonk, but the proud bishop could not forgive him, did not want to ordain him. And again he endured everything, and did not leave his monastery. Of course each of the ascetics carries himself in his own way. But did it really reach such a hatred that murder of one's own brother was contemplated?! And even in a monastery! God forbid! I know, I remember that good, kind monks would persuade novices not to strive to go to city monasteries. Yes, and those who would move there indeed endured great calamities!

The Athonite Elder Schemamonk Silouan says that he knew people who would come to Athos being good and pure, and later would be corrupted. Yes, such sad things did happen, too. I entered St. Tikhon's Monastery on the 17th of June, 1906. On the left cliros among the singers there was a ryassaphore monk, Father Gregory. Some older monks would say to me: "This is our future ascetic. He is humble and meek. Learn from him, stay close to him." Yes, it was true, Father Gregory was indeed as if an old monk-ascetic. And I visited him, had talks with him. But then I heard time and again that Father Gregory began to drink now and then. Then I saw him in trapeza making prostrations publicly. And later, even sadder, his contact with a village girl. He was handsome, tall, and blond. Oh, how one feels sorry for such ones!! Then one winter day he came to me and said: "Brother Michael, I am leaving the monastery. I am being expelled and you know why. I am going to Moscow." And then he so pitifully, painfully exclaimed: "Oh, Misha, how hard it is for me! I feel so bad, but what can I do? It is vodka that drove me to my fall. Pray for me and do not judge me. I know that you always loved me; you visited me." He left, and I went and wept bitterly. From November I received from him only one letter from Moscow.

Here is another case. A ryassaphore monk, Monk Tikhon Chernykh, had been on obedience in the prosphora bakery. He had a beautiful bass voice. Occasionally he liked to sing secular songs. Of course he did that either in the woods or in his cell with the window closed. He was a simple, kind man. But occasionally he used to drink. Once he felt the urge to go to Moscow, to the Lavra [of St. Sergius of

Radonezh]. Later we heard that Tikhon Chernykh was for a while well off there; he became a singer in the Lavra. Then one day we read in the newspapers that in the Holy Trinity Lavra an elder had been killed, a hieromonk, and that several novices had been arrested, among them Tikhon Chernykh. The trial dragged on for a long time. And this is what happened. Several singer-novices had a drinking party. Tikhon Chernykh was among them. One of the lay guards there decided to kill an old hieromonk, thinking that he had a lot of money. But as he was getting ready to do the criminal deed, he saw Fr. Tikhon's cell door open, and he took his boots and went in them to perform his evil deed. Having accomplished his bloody deed, the murderer returned, took off the bloody boots, and left them in Father Tikhon's cell. They brought search dogs from Moscow who led the police to the cell of Fr. Tikhon, and of course he was taken to Moscow, to a prison, where he suffered for two years. Now I don't remember how they discovered the real guilty ones in this terrible case. But I do remember that once I was walking on Nikita Street in Tula and I heard: "My dear Misha, is it you?" And I saw a poor old peasant. He had aged terribly, his stoutness was gone, and he was poorly dressed. He was then returning to St. Tikhon's Monastery, to his "Father's house." This is what sometimes happens with us monks.

I began to recall much, reading the book on Elder Gabriel. And many names of my own acquaintances I saw in the book, who were his admirers; of course they are now all dead. From what I heard in St. Peter's Monastery in Moscow, there were always monks from Optina Monastery there. I heard that in 1914, fifty years ago. But what amazed me was what envy people have, even monks. I also envied those who had a kind, good personality.

How truly one poet [Nikitin] said:

Judge not! It's not that people's souls are truly mean,
Their quality of life is often bad,
At first find out what sorrows they have seen
And tragedies that made their life so sad.

Yes, it is true; it often happens that the life of some people is so cruel. There is for you another ascetic, our blessed elder Hieroschema-monk Theophilus, who was hated by his own mother. And further on, one trouble after another followed for this wonderful chosen one of God. It is hardly possible to withhold tears, reading his much-suffering life.

St. Herman's Relics to be Kept at Spruce Island Hermitage

In 1939, the Platonites decided to canonize Elder Father Herman. They even wrote a service to him and an akathist.* Then Bishop Jonah asked me on Spruce Island: "Father Gerasim, where do you think it is better to serve the festivities to Elder Herman?" I answered him: "I think it would be more convenient to have them in Kodiak, where the Elder spent many years. Also, to get to Spruce Island is not always possible at any given time; the place is very stormy. Besides, there is nothing here. This is not Russia, where there were millions of believing Orthodox people, where there were many kind rich people. Of course, the relics of Elder Father Herman could be brought there for a time." In their malice the Leontyites armed themselves against the canonization of our luminary, holy righteous Father John of Kronstadt.... People wrote to me that their priests criticized those who wrote glorifying Elder Father Herman. They are all [old] Platonites. Do such need the canonization of the Elder of God, prophet of God, the great miracle-worker Father John?! They were correctly called by Archbishop Vitaly [Maximenko] "business men." Oh, how sorrowful is this church division!!! I have grieved over it all these years since 1926.

---

*We could never find these anywhere.

Soon it will be midnight, I am still writing to you this sorrowful letter. News from Palestine that our holy places were given over to the Reds forced me to suffer again. Oh, how hard it is to labor in the vineyard of the Church. If only I were a bit stronger, I would be able to split wood, then I would run away to my beloved hermitage. But I am old and sick. But all is in God's hands. Yes, something terrible is going on over the whole world.

It's midnight. At this hour on Mt. Athos monk-elders are praying for the whole world. I love that wonderfully divine Athos! Forgive me.

Afognak

Today is the 4/17th of December, the day of the Great Martyr Barbara. I was consoled by the fact that the *New Dawn* [Novaya Zarya] stated that it is not true about our holy places in holy Palestine. Glory be to God!!! For I was visited by a sinful depression. Nowadays troubles are pouring on us from all sides. I received a letter from Europe, and everyone is writing about their sorrowful life. But here my Aleuts drink a lot, having a good time, while the earth still quakes at times. At least today it is quiet and not cold at all. In December at times the water rises very high, and we all were afraid of the north winds that cause trouble, and of high waves.

The Afognak village and all its inhabitants have been moved to a new place. What remained in Afognak will be burned. I am sad!!! I lived and worked there for eighteen years. I feel sorry for the cemetery where hundreds of my spiritual children lie. Before the Second World War on many crosses there were lamps and icons and holy vigil-lights—lampadas. I love that very much.

In 1914 at the end of April I visited a women's convent "Joy and Consolation." It was built on a high bank of the Oka River, and the view from the balcony of the guesthouse was splendid!!! In the evening, sitting on the balcony, I saw a multitude of little lights that glittered behind lilac bushes and birch trees. I was drawn there; I came down, walked a little and saw a beautiful picture! In the monastery graveyard there shone hundreds of multicolored lampadas. O Lord, what beauty that was!!! I remember, I did not even want to leave that wonderful little holy place!!*

I love the flickering of this holy light; I have loved it since my childhood days! Yes, it was loved by all believing Russian people. And over the grave, over the stone slab of the Eldress Blessed Xenia, there were suspended a multitude of lampadas. I do not like electricity in church. No, I do not! I love lampadas, wax candles. Remember how good it was in the large chapel on the 14th/27th of August, on the eve of the feast day of the Dormition of the Theotokos?! Last summer on the 14th it was pouring rain. But nevertheless I served and was delighted. I love that feast day.

I don't know for certain where you are now. I am sending this letter to the old address, 355 Monroe St., Monterey, California. I brought the earth of Elder Herman to Ouzinkie. Tell me where to send the package. I am sending regards to your close ones. I pray for you and yours.

Forgive me. I don't write well. I have not been feeling well, especially since the 27th of March, 1964. I will hardly live up to May 4th, 1965, when I will celebrate the 50th anniversary of my life in the land of the New World. Also, fifty years of my priesthood. Of course, I'll spend it with prayer to God, the Mother of God, and the Saints of God. I keep praying for the friends of Elder Father Herman [the Yanovsky family] who are buried in my native Kaluga diocese.

I greet you all with the feast of Christ's Nativity.

Yours in soul,
A. Gerasim

---

*It was founded by Abbess Sophia, later of Kiev. See I. M. Andreyev, *Russia's Catacomb Saints* (Platina, California: St. Herman of Alaska Brotherhood, 1982), pp. 348-357; and the Russian-language *Russian Pilgrim*, No. 16, 1997, pp. 122-143.

Convent of Joy and Consolation, established by Abbess Sophia, later of the
Kiev Protection Convent, which was visited by Fr. Gerasim
en route to Mt. Athos in 1911.

Abbess Sophia of Kiev.

Protection Convent in Kiev.

LETTER 14
January 22, 1965

Deeply respected Gleb Dimitrievich,

The mercy of God be with you!

Today is already the 7th/20th of January, 1965. So the holy days of the Feast [Christmas] have gone by. This year the holidays came and went and I spent them sadly. All that time the sea was stormy, the wind boisterous, and it was cold up until Orthodox Christmas. My people, parishioners—it seems they forgot what took place on the 27th of March [1964]. They continue to drink and behave outrageously. But what I see from the press, it is no better in the whole world. The New Year, according to the new style, our Orthodox Russians met pleasing Satan up and down, in various clubs where drinks flowed like a river. There was a wonderful article by Archbishop Averky printed in *Orthodox Russia,* but it remained a voice in the wilderness. But thanks be to God that the noise in "Joy of All Who Sorrow" parish stopped. I took these years of strife very painfully. Of course, this is the work of the evil satan.

Something similar used to happen in Tsarist Russia also. When Archbishop Evdokim began building a church in the city of Tula, then there followed an uproar raised by the diocesan bishop and the priests. The affair reached the Synod. It was sad that it took place in an Orthodox country. But here, where all kinds of people have gathered and many are already infected with the air of a sectarian country, our Russians decided to take command over hierarchs and presbyters. While the Lord gave us a righteous hierarch, a man of prayer as was Archbishop Tikhon....

Oh, what a sorrowful summer I spent in the hermitage in 1964! And that terrible earthquake, the destruction of old parishes—all that undermined my health. Just think, Afognak, where I spent eighteen years, all perished; everything there is gone! And there was a wonderful church with good icons. One of them, the Mother of God "Joy and Consolation," I ordered from Mount Athos. It was masterfully done. I grieve over my Hermitage of Elder Father Herman!

I am seventy-six years old. My health is bad, and my sight failing.

*A Poem for Father Gerasim**
BY MICHAEL VINOKOUROFF

... And over where he lay, some men erected
An altar with a church and went away.
And to the laws of time it was subjected
Till all was left in dust and in decay.

> And meanwhile, much was written: some proposed
> To build a monastery (so they thought).
> Troparions, Akathists were composed—
> The ruin of the chapel they forgot.

Through storms, in snow, in violent winter weather,
The church was wrecked and lay in disrepair,
Without a caring hand to keep together,
Preserve, protect the holy objects there.

> And then, directed by the Higher Power,
> You, a true monastic, came and fell
> Before the Saint that memorable hour,
> And, having prayed, with him you chose to dwell.

None but you, without a friendly word
From those who should have helped you in your plight,
And with no worldly praise or gain procured,
Have lit the lamp within the depth of night.

---

*For the complete text of this poem, see *Fr. Gerasim of New Valaam,* pp. 57–58.

And now you're weak, with little time to live;
A dream, blown in from Athos, murmurs low.
Your heart, I know, is warm and sensitive
When pangs of gentle sorrow come and go.

Through storms, in snow, in violent winter weather,
The church was wrecked and lay in disrepair,
Without a caring hand to keep together,
Preserve, protect the holy objects there.

I heard that they are dreaming to take away the relics of Elder Father Herman to New York. Yes, they were hoping to "make business" with his holy remains. But such a thing is a blasphemy!! Elder Father Herman belongs to Orthodox Alaska. He struggled here for his salvation for over forty years, and his place is Spruce Island Hermitage. And now, most sorrowful it is that those who were gathering dollars to build a monastery here have done nothing and built nothing! Yes, they even attempted to banish me with all kinds of lies. But, glory be to God, I have lived here already thirty years and love my desert hermitage.

During the Christmas holidays, in my free time I again reread new books that Holy Trinity Monastery has published in these last years: *Fool-for-Christ's-Sake Hieroschemamonk Theophilus,* Elder Archimandrite Symeon on *Elder Schema-Archimandrite Gabriel of Spaso-Eleazar Monastery* [Pskov and Kazan]. Yes, it is true that in Russia they would tonsure into the mantia [stavrophore] as if it were an award. And I know that because of the caprice of older ones, the young ones were indeed bypassed, and this caused evil. Only on Mount Athos did I find that he who wishes to be tonsured requests this of the abbot. But only good father-confessors and elders did not bless [ryassaphore monks or novices] to leave their monastery because of that [that is, for not being tonsured]. Those who left would be unfortunate in life. But sorrow, anger, slander—they are everywhere and always. In Optina there were such great luminaries as that wonderful Elder Joseph. He was meek, gentle, loving everyone. But in monasteries there really were also evil men, slanderers. But who can escape them? Look how much Elder Theophil suffered! And from his own brothers!

Afterwards, I reread also about Blessed Xenia. O Lord, what great saints there used to be in Russia!! I had heard about her since my childhood years. In September 1914, I visited her grave. There was a lovely chapel. She was venerated by the whole of Russia.

I read in the newspaper that you are selling Mount Athos incense. I ask you to send me, well, at least $10.00 worth. And if you still have more little icons of St. Tikhon of Kaluga, then I ask you to send me one. The one from you I sent to a sick Russian lady who in 1916 fled from Poland and lived near St. Tikhon's Monastery. This is my dear Saint of God from my native places. I know, I heard often, that our bishops and father-archimandrites in their sermons remember their own academies. But we, simple monks, love to reminisce about our monasteries, where we placed the beginning of our monastic life. Oh, how close it is to the soul of a monk! And they were dear even to those, who because of evil people, were deprived of their monasteries! But the Lord never gave me a chance to see again my holy mother-monastery!! Yet I managed to help, although not many, those who were expelled by the Bolsheviks. I loved and love monasteries and monasticism.

Father Ambrose Konovalov is now in the rank of archimandrite. And Father Macarius* also, but he is already old. Besides, Father Ambrose does not see too well. From Mount Athos for a long time now no one has written to me; only the old and sick remain there.

Thank you for a wonderful gift. I received it on the 24th of December, old style—in the evening. Thank you. I'm sending greetings to your mother and Ia.

---

*A schemamonk from Mt. Athos who lived for a while with Fr. Gerasim on Monks' Lagoon in the dilapidated beach house. See *New Valaam on Monks' Lagoon*, Platina, 1997, pp. 44 and 47.

HIEROSCHEMAMONK MACARIUS (KOCYBINSKY).
In his Protection Skete in Bluffton, Alberta, Canada.
I photographed him in October, 1961.

Today is the 8th/21st of January. It is damp. Fog. Yesterday the [high tide] water level was high. A northwest wind is blowing, and the shore is quite washed away. Such a thing makes me nervous, and I slept badly. And today there is something wrong with my stove, it does not burn. Here is contemporary civilization for you! It's not like the little Russian-house, ceramic stove, where it was so cozy, warm, even in terrible freezing temperatures. And our houses out of pine logs stood for centuries. But of course, as they say, each crow praises its nest. Now in Russia, too, they build these new houses, "modern" ones, where both water and people freeze. In *Russian Life* there were good articles recently where our people remember Tsarist Russia with kind words. In reading such a thing one's soul rejoices—one tear after another runs down.

Forgive me that I don't seem to get busy and send you the earth from the grave of Elder Father Herman. I wrote to you before the American holiday that the cold and stormy weather lasted for quite a while. On such days I cannot write; it is cold in my apartment. I do not know whether there be any priests or monks in America who have suffered so much from cold during these forty-nine years!

On May 4th of this 1965 will be fifty years of my service in the North American diocese.

Our bishops are all monks, and, according to the vows given to God, cannot gather gold, silver, or have real estate. But he, Metropolitan Platon, left a store house to his daughter Barbara, and for money gave out mitres to rich monks. But for such people anything is possible. What amazes me is how such people do not fear God and the judgment of God?! Besides, they are already old people.

Oh, how difficult it is to work in the vineyard of God! It is true that our Mother the Orthodox Church never did take the crown of thorns from Her head. The persecution of archpastors, pastors, and monks also took place during the Tsarist regime. But now the times of Antichrist have come. One well-educated and believing lady wrote to me from Yugoslavia: "One does not have to be a prophet in order to know what will be on our earthly globe in twenty to forty years. One does not now see youth in church...." The Lord called her to Himself. She was a Russian patriot, suffering in her soul for our Mother Russia.

I read in *New Dawn* that Archbishop John Shakhovskoy went to Europe and other places. And, of course, for propaganda. He wrote to me some time ago. I did not answer him. He is running around with Catholics. And they are sly and cunning—even to this day.

I saw on a photograph the new "Joy of All Who Sorrow" Cathedral. An imposing edifice! May the Lord send peace and holy love among our Christians.

The rain still continues to pour!

I'm sending greetings to your co-brothers. May Christ protect you.

Yours in soul,
Archim. Gerasim

LETTER 15
April 6, 1965

Dear Gleb Dimitrievich,

I'm sending you greetings from Alaska! Today is March 22/April 4; the sun shines but it is cold. Forgive me for my long silence. But you also seem to be somewhat stingy in writing. I received two envelopes with the magazine *The Orthodox Word.* Our cathedral appears to be beautiful, and still some are hissing in disdain. All should be rejoicing and thanking God for it.

A year has passed by since the 27th of March when the Lord visited our sinful planet, and He visited it sternly, assuredly. I still, whenever I hear some sort of noise, at once think: "Earthquake!" And, although I am sick and have had ailing nerves for a long time, yet since the 27th of March, 1964, I am no longer the same. I am weak in everything, everywhere, both in my legs and eyes. I am disintegrating. But it is time; I am already seventy-six years old. On the 4th of May I will have been in exile and suffering for half a century. This terrible occurrence that took place on March 27th, 1964, did not wisen us up at all. As I see it, people have only become worse. But something similar keeps going on throughout the whole world.

I am sorry for my quiet hermitage, that now I am old and feeble and am not able to work there as I did ten years ago. And these Platonite bishops have done nothing good for Elder Father Herman. Bishop Alexey Panteleev gathered donations for it, $3,000, and not a cent went for this good deed [building a monastery]. And another, Metropolitan Leonty, answered to my dismay: "Bishop Alexey was practicing!" O my God, where is man's conscience!?!! Yet they are supposed to be learned people, academicians.

In Russia, in the Kaluga diocese, there was a simple elder, Father Gerasim,* who in only six years built a wonderful monastery. There was a beautiful church, monastery buildings, a wooden fence. It was similar to our ancient Russia. But Father Gerasim was a true monk and a lover of monasticism! He served Liturgy in such a way that he forced people to pray. He was of tall stature. He had a good voice. Yes, and he served very well. I used to love to visit his monastery; it was dedicated to St. Sergius of Radonezh. I always remember the words of Metropolitan Gabriel, written to the Abbot of Sarov Monastery: "I have many wise people myself in Petersburg; send me your fool, Father Nazary." What would you think?! Father Nazary in a short time transformed poor Valaam into a wonderful Lavra!!! Should a true Valaam monk come to Spruce Island, he would have built there a real skete. Now Russian monks are not striving to seclude themselves in a quiet monastery, to which we belong according to our monastic vows. And that is very pitiful!

In Russia all our monasteries are destroyed, and there the Godless atheists are persecuting monks, they are torturing them. And all this is sent to us for our sins. One of my friends, a monk, visited St. Tikhon's Monastery in June of 1916. He visited it with Bishop Juvenal, who was

---

*See Appendix II below.

then travelling to Schema-Archimandrite Gabriel in Kazan. He wrote to me: "All monks there are fighting, cursing each other!!" Well, they received their just desserts. The Bolsheviks treated them mercilessly, ferociously; they chased them out of Kaluga to forced labor. And several of them ended their lives in that way. Others went to prison, while others to Siberia. But I, a former resident of St. Tikhon's Monastery, feel very sorry for them and co-suffered with them. Oh, how beautiful was St. Tikhon's Monastery!!! It is difficult to forget. I left it at the end of August, 1911, and never again was I able to visit it. I really had no time, for I worked in Tula in the huge Church of the Protection of the Mother of God. Then I didn't think that I would be in America. But in the beginning of the World War a certain depression visited me, a certain forboding that something frightening would take place in Russia. And the same feeling wouldn't leave me when I was in Petrograd, where I spent that winter.

In Petrograd there were many of our national holy places where I often withdrew for prayer. I visited the grave of Blessed Xenia as well as the sepulchre of Righteous Father John of Kronstadt, and many [other] famous places. There I would often meet monks from Mount Athos, where we would remember that wondrous peninsula, Athos.

Archbishop Tikhon often recalled this Mount Athos, grieving over the fact that he was not in a monastery. And see, the Lord vouchsafed him to die in a holy monastery, and to have such a wonderful death. But still, Russian Mount Athos is passing away, and such a thing makes me very sad. O Athos, my priceless Athos!! There never was or is such a place on the earth.

I read in the newspaper that the Leontyites have already begun the practice of "general confession." Believe me, such a thing will demoralize the young generation completely. I confessed Russian youth, although not for a long time. But I know that they all did repent for their own sins and that they repented whole-heartedly. It is true, though, that they do not want to repent of their serious sins. St. John of Kronstadt is a different case; the human soul was open before him. He knew quite well how our Russian people repented. This general confession simply frightens me. I know that our intelligentsia of little faith have for a long time now rejected it [confession].

I read recently that Archimandrite Peter Zaichenko, being in a hospital and preparing himself to die, summoned a barber to shave him before he died. I was struck by that!!! I worked in monastery infirmaries and remember how our monks used to die. Then each sick monk cared only for his soul and tried to prepare it for passing to the other world. Now all are striving to change, to pervert, what has come to us, our 2,000-year inheritance. After all, sin is a sickness of the soul. And how can a priest who confesses hundreds of people in a moment heal a sick soul?! In Russia our simple fold never even heard of such sins which even our school children in America know about! Even here in Alaska, also. Oh, no! I was struck by such a novelty as general confession. But of course contemporary youth wants just that. If during confession we do not repent of frightful sins such as fornication, adultery, and other fleshly sins, then we are receiving Communion unto judgment and condemnation. Our Christian body is a temple of God, and the Holy Apostle Paul says that whoever defiles the temple of God, his body, with such sins, the Lord will punish. A priest is a spiritual physician, and how can he heal your soul if you conceal from him its sickness? When you go to a doctor to heal your body, do you conceal your pains? Think of what you are saying. It is as if you drank a glass of wine or vodka! The sacrament of penance was established by God Himself. Of course, I told people much about St. John of Kronstadt, how he chastized those who hid their sins from false fear. Ah, everything today becomes different.

I remember how once a young peasant entered our monastery. Having come into church and gone into the choir loft, I saw him in a corner, bitterly weeping. Of course, I felt sorry for him. I came up to him and asked: "Who hurt you? What are you crying about?" And he answered me: "Forgive me, no one hurt me; I am crying over my sins." Such a thing touched me, and I felt contrition in my heart from his answer. Is it possible to find something similar in our evil times?! One man told me how his grandfather, a peasant, taught him to do the mental Jesus prayer.

Yes, my dear, there were times in Holy Russia when our lay people indeed seriously prayed the Jesus prayer. I remember that often, and am praying to the Lord and to such ascetics that He, the Lord, might save our Russian homeland. Our suffering people!! But many of our Russian people have already forgotten their motherland....

In the Metropolia they didn't tell you the truth that they did not collect or record the miracles of Elder Herman. O Lord!!! What lies!!! Bishop Alexey Panteleev recorded and gathered them from all parishes in the Alaskan diocese. And Bishop Ambrose finally came to his senses and wrote his plea to the clergy, calling them to work in the Orthodox vineyard of Alaska. I do not know whether the spoiled priests will answer his plea....

Today is the fifth in the new style. It is overcast, damp. In the evening I intend to read the Great Canon of St. Andrew, Bishop of the island of Crete. I love it very much. I repent by its words of contrition. But I hear that the earthquake continues across the whole world. Yet our people have a cold attitude toward all that. The people's hearts have become coarse.... I'm going to trim the lamps.

Today is the 24th of March, old style. Today is the day of the repose of my aunt, Nun Angelina, in the world Alexandra Giorgievna Schmaltz. She secluded herself in a monastery, being already in old age, but she had lived in the world like a nun.

Today we have stormy, cold weather, but there is no snow. It is only the mountains that are covered with it.

I cannot understand the title "proto-presbyter." It is a Greek word and designates archpriest. During the service of elevation into that rank, the bishop says: "This presbyter is raised to proto-presbyter." This was invented by the Tsars, laymen, and is unlawful, just as unlawful as when we had laymen-oberprocurators, who had command over the hierarchs. The head of the Church of Christ must be a spiritual authority—a patriarch. It is true that some of them were unbelievers, and very many of our good hierarchs suffered a lot and even died prematurely. Then God gave us a good father, His Holiness Patriarch Tikhon, a meek man, the kindest, a true monk, and such a good man was given over to tortures by his own false brothers!!! He was tormented not only by Bolsheviks, but he was betrayed by our learned hierarchs, priests and monks! I read a "Living Church" journal and was shocked at the hatred with which his former friends wrote about him. Some people wrote to me about that, too. But I could not write there in his defense, for my letters were opened there. Of course, would my words, those of a simple, unlearned monk, bring any good to such evil people? Although they were all learned, educated, they were the ones who also slandered the Tsar-martyr—defamed and slandered.

Once in 1913 Archbishop Evdokim invited a photographer, and he photographed our Protection Cathedral with various shots. The photographs came out very well. He had an album made with these pictures and sent it to the Tsar. The Tsar in gratitude sent an icon of St. Nicholas of exquisite artistry. Then we had a great celebration; two archbishops served, and there were a lot of people. There was a military parade and music. Then Archpastor Evdokim, who often spoke about the emperor, highly praised him, but after his abdication he was against him and used to say: "Nicholas Romanov never liked me, because I told him the truth." Poor, poor Bishop Evdokim, when did you do that?! Perhaps in your dreams? Oh, how sad was their end!! Forgive me. I cannot any more recollect or remember it, it pains my soul!

Well, it is time to end. Today is the 26th of March, old style, and it is cold. It blows northerly. All the news is awful, the earth trembles from our sins. I do not feel too well. My eyesight is failing, but I still serve and work. It is hard for me to work because my strength dissipates. I miss my hermitage, where I would wish to spend the days of Great Lent. Forgive me.

Your
A. Gerasim

LETTER 16
February 23, 1966

My dear Gleb Dimitrievich,

The mercy of God be with you!

Forgive me for my long silence, but I have not served for more than two months. I have high blood pressure and my heart is not well. In cold weather I cannot be exposed to fresh air; a pain begins, a sharp pain in my left arm, and the pain goes to my chest. When I received pills from the doctor, it subsided. Even then at times it seizes me and I can hardly get home. I am already seventy-seven years old and six months. And the life here in Alaska has gotten worse. The old-timers who liked everything Russian have all died out, and the new generation is proud now, self-loving, obstinate. They are free-thinkers. My apartment is cold, the wind penetrates through all the cracks. The wind here at times is cruel. Since the 27th of March, 1964, the weather has been almost always stormy.

I like orderliness in church, cleanliness, but it is hard for me now to work. Alas, as the saying goes, "High hills have tired out my horse!"

I thank you for a beautiful Christmas icon card. But I would not advise you to use an icon of the Mother of God, a copy of the wonderworking Kazan Icon of the Mother of God, making a Christmas card out of it. Now not only the heterodox, but also many of our Russian Orthodox, have begun to have a flippant attitude towards holy icons. Now I see that this icon of the Kazan Mother of God is very ancient. I see what an artful work the precious riza is. In the last years before the World War (I), our craftsmen would masterfully adorn these rizas for icons. They were true artists of this craft. In Petrograd in the church of the Athonite Metochion there was a wonderworking icon of the Mother of God "Consolation in Sorrows and Grief," and with what a wonderful riza it was bedecked! And others that I had chanced to see were wonderful. I am an admirer of them. Every time, in visiting a church, I love to admire the wonderful work of our masters.

In St. Tikhon's Monastery there was a wonderful Vladimir Icon of the Mother of God which was adorned with a pearl riza. Even up to today I remember its beauty, its art.

At the homes of our rich merchants, religious people, there were icons decorated with rizas of precious stones. It is possible that this icon which is now in America belonged to a wealthy Russian man. The aunt of my father also had icons bedecked with pearls and precious stones. Russian people, the believing folk, used to simply love to decorate icons with rizas, especially icons of the Theotokos. I also love holy icons. On Mount Athos all miracle-working icons have precious rizas, gifts of the Russian people.

On the 18th of February I received a letter from Russia. There, on the 16th of February, at six in the evening, my last brother Nicholas died, being seventy-five years old. He had been sick since last autumn, and spent the Christmas holidays in bed. He was kind and a believer. Of course, I have been grieving these days. Now, out of all my relatives there remains only my sister Vera, eighty years old. In our town, Alexin of the Tula region, the cemetery is closed. The church also. That makes me sad. The Bolsheviks closed the cemeteries. They removed all gravestones, crosses, chapels. There all my close ones, my relatives, lie buried, and also all our priests. O Lord, how sad it is! They don't give rest even to the dead bones there. I recall in Odessa I saw a closed cemetery. No one touched the bones of the ones buried there then. This is what we get with our "freedom." My brother was buried in a new cemetery, somewhere on the other side of the Oka River, that was then already part of the Kaluga region. Now they have mined everything. Everywhere frightful things are going on. But Russian people of all classes had a premonition about the trouble coming to Russia way before 1914. Archbishop Nikon, formerly of Vologda, spoke much about that. Others did, also.

Vera Alexandrovna Balashova, Fr. Gerasim's sister,
photographed in Alexin, his hometown.

It is now the first week of Great Lent, and I am not serving. The weather is very cold. I'm reading at home the Great Canon of St. Andrew, bishop of Crete. I love it very much. Archbishop Evdokim used to read it very well, with great expression, and the singing was wonderful. But, of course, nowhere were there days spent as in monasteries.

Not so long ago I received a postcard view of St. Tikhon's Monastery, and seeing it my soul cried out with moaning. The man who sent it to me was born in Kaluga. While still a child his parents took him to Harbin [Manchuria], where he lived until 1922. When he was fourteen years old, his parents visited their native land, and also St. Tikhon's Monastery. But then I was already living in Tula. Yet, seeing the photos of my dear St. Tikhon's Monastery, tears ran down my face involuntarily. Just think, that monastery is no longer there! And much else is now already torn down, destroyed. Of course that man has no idea what is left there of the past. Some twenty years ago my friend and countryman, having spent twelve years in Sibera, returned to Russia and visited his native places. He regretted that he visited his former monastery. By now, probably, all its monks have left for the other world.* Kaluga also suffered quite a bit during the years of the Second World War. Its last abbot, Father Jonah, died in prison.

How do you like the new cathedral [in San Francisco]? Again they fight, now about the old "Joy of All Who Sorrow" Cathedral. Of course, it is true people prayed there for many years, wept over their sorrows, their misfortunes. And Archbishop Tikhon served there, prayed there. He was a great ascetic, a man of prayer. Also there was Archpriest Basil Shaposhnikoff.** It has now become hard to labor in the vineyard of

---

*Now, however, the monastery is being restored, bit by bit, by a zealous Abbot Tikhon, and services are conducted in the former infirmary where Fr. Gerasim lived and had his obedience as an orderly during his novitiate.

** He had a righteous death. On Monday of Great Lent, as he came down from the altar, quite healthy, to the nave of the cathedral to start reading the Great Canon, he read the first verse: "Where shall I begin to weep?"—and fell down and died.

God! And here in America the white clergy do not like monks. Once a celibate priest wrote to me, being lonely, also: "Monks hurt us." Now he is dead. I heard such a thing from my first day in America. But the priests do not want to come to Alaska to work in a cold land; yet there was a time when educated priests and bishops, academy graduates, labored here.

You, of course, heard that the cathedral in Sitka burned down. Here in Alaska two churches have burned! In Kodiak the Resurrection Church, and in Sitka St. Michael's Cathedral. In Kodiak all icons, all of the valuable church vessels, perished. It was also a cathedral. A large beautiful chalice perished and ancient blessing crosses. Father Macary Baranoff wrote that a valuable vestry of vestments burned, too. No, it is not true. All the vestments were worn out and in rags. I lived in Sitka for four months, and I know that in that cathedral much also had been stolen. Oh, it's better to be silent. The Platonites defend their own people. Still, in 1915 I saw certain things in the New York Cathedral which rightly belonged to the Sitka Cathedral.

Judging from a photo, I do not like the new Metropolitan Ireney. I read in the newspaper that he flew to Belgium for a meeting with Archbishop Gregory [Moscow Patriarchate].

Just look what episcopal hatred does!! I remember a rhymned saying uttered by a simple monk:

«Архіерейская злоба — до гроба».

Archpastors rant and rave,
Won't stop until their grave.

From 1901 until 1917, the Kaluga diocese was headed by Bishop Benjamin. He was of tall stature, served well, read expressively, and nearby him was always a still rather young woman, his aunt. One hierodeacon, who was his prosphora baker, did not want to live any longer at the archpastoral residence. He chose for himself a poor monastery, still a rather new one, St. Sergius Hermitage. The elder-abbot of that monastery was Hieromonk Gerasim, who presented him to the bishop to be ordained a hieromonk. But the bishop sternly declared: "As long as I occupy the Kaluga diocese, he will not be a hieromonk." And that is how it turned out. But that hierodeacon was a modest monk; he never said anything bad about the bishop, and he chose for himself a poor, deserted monastery. That hierarch, Benjamin Muratovsky, after the Revolution joined the Renovationists and died in schism in 1930. He was formerly a widowed priest of the Kazan diocese. He was a proud man and never conversed with monks.

Today is overcast, the 23rd of February. It snows. But glory be to God, it is quiet. It is already Wednesday of the First Week of Lent. As my kind elder, Schemamonk Ioasaph, would say, "We have set sail." He died from starvation on the 2nd of January in 1919, when all monks were already cleared out of St. Tikhon's Monastery. He was a holy monk! Forgive me. I'm sending greetings to your relatives and your co-strugglers.

Sincerely yours,
A. Gerasim

LETTER 17
July 22, 1966

Your honor, dear brother in Christ Jesus, Gleb!

Today is July 22, new style, but there is no news from you. I sent to you my donation of $25.00 for the publication of *The Orthodox Word*. Both the letter and the money order were sent to the address of the magazine. It was also sent certified. We had a stormy winter, spring and beginning of summer. I am meanwhile in Ouzinkie. My legs have become weak; I cannot walk far. And life becomes harder and harder. I am almost seventy-eight years old.

Archbishop John indeed had a blessed repose! It is sad to see luminaries of Christ's Church leave for the other world in such frightful times as ours. I remember while in Russia believing people used to say when our righteous ones, our luminaries, would die: "Evidently something terrible will occur in Russia, for the Lord is calling to Himself his righteous ones, people of deep prayer." Yes, that's how it was: a righteous man died, and in his place there was no other righteous one to replace him! The same is occurring now also outside of our native Russian land.

The prayer of Athonite monastics is also dying out. Their monasteries have become deserted, turned into empty places without monk-ascetics, whose presence used to adorn the Holy Mountain for more than a thousand years. Elder Silouan used to say: "We are the last Russian monks." O Lord, save us and Thy whole world! Yes, something terrible is going on throughout the whole world. From Soviet Russia I have not received a letter since January 26th. There the persecution of God, Christ, and Orthodoxy is still going on, while Patriarch Alexey and his faithful servants are still defending the Godless authority and go against our believers and confessors. Monasteries there are closed, both men's and women's, and also many Orthodox churches. Probably there are no more monks from Tsarist times....

In the beginning of September it will be fifty years of my serving in Alaska. I am abandoned here, there are no Russians. I am old, sick, but I miss Russia often, shedding tears. Oh, how beautiful was our native Russia!!! Just think, I remember old Russia, when there was a white Tsar on the throne!

Write to me, do not forget me.

Am sending my regards to yours.

May the Lord keep you!

Yours in spirit,
Archim. Gerasim

ARCHBISHOP JOHN OF SHANGHAI AND SAN FRANCISCO,
reposed in 1969 and recently canonized, was co-founder with Fr. Gerasim
of the St. Herman Brotherhood. Although they never met,
they were of the same spirit.

LETTER 18
October 18, 1966

Dear Brother Gleb and your Brothers in Christ Jesus,

I am sending you my greetings from Kodiak, where I arrived on the 6th of September, new style. Your kind letter of the 8th of September, old style, was received by me. I arrived in Kodiak in order to visit the eye doctor (optometrist), because my vision is getting weaker. It is time to change my glasses. My vision declined after the frightful earthquake. Forgive me. Presently I am unable to send you anything from Spruce Island Hermitage—I have not been there for quite some time. My legs have become weak; I am unable to walk far. And I sorrow for my quiet hermitage. From the day of that horrible earthquake the sea almost all the time is stormy, and the wind northwest. During the summer months everyone is working, and there is no one to get me to the eastern side of the island. And to walk from Pestrikoff Beach I am no longer able, alas! I think, too, that in these years the river beavers have flooded the streams, making it difficult to reach my little hermitage.

I remember what I wrote to you about the prophecy of St. Seraphim, Wonderworker of Sarov: "In the last times, many Orthodox bishops will fall into heresy. I, lowly Seraphim, have prayed for them, but the Lord did not hear my prayers...." I, sinful Monk Gerasim, heard some terrible things from the lips of a bishop. I do not know if he ever repented; he was sent a great trial. After all, the Lord pardoned both robbers and fornicators.

One archpriest, an educated and wise man, having visited Mount Athos, St. Elias Skete, in his sermon said why the Lord punished our Russia and our people. He said a shocking thing: that twenty of our bishops were atheists. Having read this letter of the Athonite monk, my soul was filled with sorrow. From early childhood I loved the hierarchi-

Inside the Kaluga Chapel with an Athonite-skete type of altar table (paraklesis), with an icon of the Kaluga Theotokos painted for Fr. Gerasim on Athos.

The beloved hermitage of Fr. Gerasim. On the left is the Kaluga Chapel; on the right is his cell. The window on the left is his bedroom, wherein is an altar table where he performed Divine Liturgy according to the Athonite manner and that of St. Theophan the Recluse.

cal church service with the bishop, considering a bishop to be not of this world. But after what that archpriest wrote—I am deeply distressed. Metropolitan Methodius, a conscientious, careful hierarch, believer, and lover of monasteries, wrote in one spiritual journal that half of our bishops were atheists—did not believe in God. O Lord, how frightful such a thing is!!!

But here is what St. Seraphim said [to Motovilov]: "Your Godliness, the Lord God has ordained that I, humble Seraphim, should live considerably longer than a hundred years. But since by that time the bishops will become so impious that in their impiety they will surpass the Greek bishops of the time of Theodosius the Younger, so that they will no longer even believe in the chief dogma of the Christian faith, therefore it has been pleasing to the Lord God to take me, humble Seraphim, from this temporal life until the time, and then resurrect me; and my resurrection will be as the resurrection of the Seven Youths in the cave of Ochlon in the days of Theodosius the Younger."*

Such a thing I heard for the first time! It is frightful!

A former Russian Consul, N.B. Bogoiavlensky, wrote to me from Seattle that there in the church hall Bishop Leonty Turkevich in his lecture denied the sanctity of St. Seraphim and St. Prince Alexander Nevsky. Also, several priests here do not revere the sanctity of the God-pleasers—the saints. I have lived in Alaska for fifty years now, and for all these long years only one archpriest, Father Elias Klopotovsky, when dying asked his wife, Matushka Maria, to send me fifty dollars. And this is all for half a century!

I read somewhere that St. Seraphim of Sarov had said that not far off was the time when the Russian people would throw down their Tsar, and when that would happen, then at once they would take down crosses from churches, bells from belltowers. And also that millions of Russians would be scattered throughout the whole world.

---

*"The Great Diveyevo Mystery," in *Little Russian Philokalia,* Vol. I, third edition (Platina, California: St. Herman of Alaska Brotherhood, 1991), p. 137.

Well? All that came true; we saw it and heard it! But the saddest part is that our Russian people living now in rich America have forgotten all that they experienced and suffered in leaving their native land. On the eves of great feast days our churches are without a congregation! And where do they spend their time? On the dance floor, pleasing satan until dawn.

Nothing like this took place in Russia before that unfortunate Revolution! I remember distinctly that in our little town Alexin in the Tula region, after the All-night Vigil I used to love to stroll the street where all was quiet, peaceful. In the houses of town folk, in their beautiful rooms that faced the street, one could see the twinkling of lampadas near their holy icons. O silent, Holy Night!!

Liturgy would be served at seven in the morning, and all of our churches were packed with people. Tula was a large city. There were many churches, and they were also diligently frequented by the faithful. Once I recall such a thing, tears involuntarily start falling on my tormented chest.

I, sinful monk Gerasim, have loved and revered St. Seraphim of Sarov from that day in 1901 when I heard his angel-like life. In 1906 I entered St. Tikhon's Monastery on the 17th of June.... In July, when I was still living in the monastery guesthouse, I was met by an orphan who worked in this guesthouse, a young man, Theodore. He met me in the corridor and in a shy, gentle way, said to me: "Misha, I have come to like you, you are always so kind to me." He was holding something in his hands. And I heard from him something joyful: "Misha, I would like to present to you this little icon." It was a little icon of St. Seraphim of Sarov. And, my God, how I rejoiced over such a gift! This icon I treasure up until this day. Everything that is written about St. Seraphim I read with awe and love. I love this God-pleaser of ours!!!

Forgive me, but I always pray for you and for your mother, sister, and the members of your Brotherhood! True, Elder Father Herman lived and labored in God's vineyard for many years in Kodiak. And for them, the God-pleasers, the saints, there is no foreign country, no kind

The Dormition Cathedral in Kaluga, built in 1813,
as it looks today being restored.

An icon of St. Seraphim
given to Fr. Gerasim by
Novice Theodore,
an orphan.

St. Herman, painted by
Archimandrite Seraphim Oblivantsev.

of visa. St. Seraphim used to say: "When I will no longer be with you, then come to me, to my grave, and the oftener the better. And falling down on my grave-site, tell me all, all your sorrows; and I will hear you and your sorrow will go away. Talk to me as if I were alive, and I am always with you." What a wonderful, touching promise. And I, sinful monk Gerasim, remember such a thing and have always run to him, all of these sixty years.

Presently I cannot send you anything from Elder Father Herman's hermitage.

Holy Apostle Paul says: "Saints are praying for us"! Oh, how true it is! Blessed Xenia was struggling for her salvation and died in Petersburg, but she helped and helps all in the whole world, whoever remembers her, as do our great wonderworkers St. Seraphim and Elder Father Herman.*

The "Great Diveyevo Mystery" which you sent me I reread ten times.**

You wrote to me that St. Seraphim told one God-fearing woman: "A catastrophe is unavoidable. Repentance is a great thing. It is pleasing to the Lord God, and the Lord in His compassion removes from us chastisement."

But where is it in our time, this repentance?! Church separation is a sinful thing. And do you think that Metropolitan Platon sorrowed over it, or Metropolitan Eulogius and their followers?! It is not apparent! No one hears about it! Metropolitan Ireney flew to Europe and made a concordat with schismatics. And nevertheless Metropolitan Platon unlawfully, by lies, took over the North American diocese. In

---

*While I was with Father Gerasim in 1961, he told me that he had read somewhere, but he did not remember where, that they had met and so knew one another. I found out that St. Herman as a 12-year-old child lived in the desert in Sarov with an old monk, Barlaam—but I learned this already after Fr. Gerasim's repose, so I could not tell him.—A. H.

** See *Little Russian Philokalia, Vol. I: St. Seraphim,* pp. 127-141.

Church affairs there cannot be any lies; Christ founded His Church on the rock of Truth.

Archbishop Alexander [Nemolovsky] wrote to me:

"Some priests write to me: 'You are at fault, because you left the diocese...' I did not leave! I accepted an offer of Metropolitan Platon to leave America for three or four months 'in order to pacify people's passions.' I did not abandon it. But hardly a month had passed when proclamations were sent out that Archbishop Alexander would not return as a ruling bishop."

Besides, Metropolitan Platon left his diocese of his own free will, taking along valuables and papers. That very night the Bolsheviks in Odessa executed by shooting more than twenty-thousand young men, who responded to the call of Metropolitan Platon and joined the army of "Holy Alliance" to save Russia. But alas, this general in a ryassa fled on a French cruiser to save his own life. I wrote this to a defender of Metropolitan Platon, Archpriest Theophanes Buketov, but he weaseled out by grave silence. Alright. We can hide all that from people, but it will not be hidden from our Lord and God.

My friends and monks from the Kaluga diocese wrote to me: "In our Monastery of St. Tikhon there were thirty hieromonks. Not one of them was trapped into renovationism, except for two who were in Siberia and were deceived there. They were told that the whole of Russia, everyone, recognized the renovationists (as legal). I can testify to all that the Kaluga ascetics, of which there are many here, defended this wonderful tucked-in monastery from heretics." And there in the Kaluga diocese many monks received martyrs' crowns. Now I don't know what takes place there in that formerly beautiful monastery.

Today is the 20th of September, old style. The sun shines brightly. But the air is cold, like autumn. I am in Kodiak, yet often in my mind I am carried to my quiet hermitage, to the grave of Elder Father Herman, where there is a different atmosphere—quiet, monastic.

The grave of Fr. Gerasim; the site he chose right from the window of his bedroom-chapel. The dark spot on the right is the site of Fr. Nicetas' cell, where he burned on Christmas day, seeing St. Herman just before that.

Fr. Gerasim in his prime, standing on the very spot where he is now buried, looking forward to the future where he beholds his long-wished-for monastic settlement on Monks' Lagoon Hermitage.

The St. Herman Brotherhood

I am very glad that your good work is progressing. May the Lord help you! But each good deed is not accomplished easily. The enemy does his work. St. Seraphim secluded himself in a deserted place in the woods, into a poor cell. But even there people (through the instigation of the enemy, the devil) cruelly beat him up and crippled him for life. And all who wish to live piously in Jesus Christ will be persecuted. Besides, keep in mind what times we live in, terrible times.

In Russia, everything has been falling apart since 1904. Many pious people of all classes used to warn about it. And now on wondrous Athos, prayer is dying off there. A newspaper wrote just now that on Mount Athos there was a terrible fire in the ancient Greek Vatopedi Monastery, where its walls had stored holy things for a thousand years. I love holy Mount Athos, and all these years I have corresponded with its monks. There is a prophecy of St. Nilus, that even this wondrous corner of the world will be deserted not long before the end of the world. Sad! But all depends on the will of God.

From your writing I am guessing that you intend to join Christ's army, to accept the monastic tonsure. And if it is so, then I rejoice for you! Be daring, do it! Oh, how I loved to be present during the rite of monastic tonsure! Bishop Evdokim when tonsuring monks would read the prayers with such warmth! He also used to deliver a wonderful homily. How amazed I was when the renovationists in their council decreed: "Shut all monasteries." And the very one who presided at that gathering was Bishop Evdokim himself! I read that when some of the members of this renovationist "sobor" were on the streets of Moscow, the faithful laymen on meeting them said: "We are believing Orthodox people; we shall never forgive you that you closed all our monasteries! We loved them!! We loved to visit them and to receive rest for our souls there within their walls." Tears like hail poured out from the eyes of those who spoke these words. Because of our sins the Lord permitted us such a fall. O Lord, forgive us. The soul aches for our Russia, for the persecuted Church of Christ!

And forgive me again for such sad writing. Oh, old age is no joy.

May Christ keep you. What you sent to me I am returning. You, too, pray for me a sinner. I do not sleep well at night.

Forgive me.

Yours in spirit,
Archim. Gerasim

Lettter 19
No Date

Your Honor, Dear Br. Gleb!

The mercy of God be with you! Your letter from the 7th of April I received in Ouzinkie a few days ago. Forgive me, so far I have not had an opportunity to fulfill your request. I am in Ouzinkie. Right now I cannot get here either water or a handful of earth from Spruce Island [Hermitage]. If I will get it, then I will send it to you without delay. I am not well. My legs torture me. At times I can barely stand on them in church during services. The last two months were spent in Kodiak where I caught the flu for the second time.

A cough was torturing me, together with congestion. Oh, in old age everything goes wrong. And if only I had firewood I would never leave my beloved desert hermitage. The news is coming from all sides, and it is all sad. And Mt. Athos, my priceless Athos, is dying out. I sorrow over this, and very much so! My sister wrote to me from Russia, Moscow. But she writes little and very cautiously. They have again raised persecution against the Church of God. But can one blame a patriarch and our suffering clergy for that?! We must pray for them, must shed tears for them. But, alas, our Russian people—despite the call of their archpastors, such as Archbishop Averky and Bishop Savva—are still as wild as demons, making masked balls on the eves of feast days, on the eves of God's days. It is sad!!!

In Russia before the Revolution, the unforgettable hierarch Archbishop Nikon, formerly of Vologda, wrote a lot, calling the Russian people to repentance; and, as the ancient people of God, he warned us of terrible times. Loving monasticism and monasteries, he taught monks much, begging them to care more about preserving their God-given vows than about the materialistic side for which they strove more: building luxurious churches, tall belfries, huge bells, luxurious buildings [in monasteries]. Hierarch Nikon was exactly right. And I know that many of our learned archpastors, educated monks, did not like Archbishop Nikon for his truthful words. And here, now people do not want to hear their archpastors, who announce the truth to them, who fight for the salvation of their souls.

And such indifference is now everywhere. And also Ouzinkie is not joyful. It is now Great Lent, and they, my Aleuts, are drinking and carousing.

On Friday during Matins I read the Akathist to the Mother of God and I wept. I read the canon. And after Matins I also served a Moleben. I also gave a sermon concerning for what occasion such a beautiful service as the service of the Laudation of the Mother of God was established. Forgive me. I will ask around, if some might have water and earth [from St. Herman's grave].

May Christ protect you. I bow to the ground before all the brothers.

Your,

A. Gerasim

APPENDIX I

A Letter of Schema-bishop Theodore (Irtel) to Brother Gleb

December 30, 1969

Christ is Born! Glorify Him!

Dear Brother Gleb,

I offer you my gratitude!

I am unable to write rational letters. For this reason I don't know if it can be of help to you....

I almost never had a chance to speak with Father Gerasim. It just turned out that way. I knew nothing about [accusations of] his fits of fear or possession and didn't hear anything about it. I know that on Afognak Island the people regarded him as a spiritual father. The Nelsons, the Sherotins and the Petelin s... would seek his advice and would strive to carry it out.... Whether they are alive and where they are I know not.... In Sitka there is a Protodeacon, Innocent Williams. (Fr. Seraphim has his address.) He knew Father Gerasim and remembers him well.

Father Gerasim only told me about his dreams in which he saw himself vested in an archpastoral mantle. This particular conversation occurred accidentally in the village of Ouzinkie when he was cleaning the church and I chanced to come in. Father Gerasim had been in correspondence with Archbishop Evdokim (Prince Meshchersky), the publisher of the magazine *The Christian,* and later bishop of Nizhni-

Novgorod, who afterwards married, stripped himself of his rank and died in the Crimea. Before his death he had confession and received the Holy Mysteries. This news consoled Father Archimandrite Gerasim. He told me that once Archbishop Evdokim was preparing to go on his usual pilgrimage with a large group of women, and while visiting a certain monastery where there was a blind, clairvoyant schemamonk, this schemamonk immediately recognized the rank of his visitor, and said: "Your Grace, do not go on pilgrimages with women. You will encounter a lot of evil with them." Bishop Evdokim did not care to hear this. He judged the schemamonk and did not listen to him.

Concerning Father Gerasim's attitude to all ecclesiastical divisions: Moscow, Synod and the American Metropolia—they were evidently all the same to him.... But he especially revered Fr. John Vostorgov.*

This is about all that is known to me abut Father Archimandrite Gerasim. He possessed a talent for writing and keen observation, which is seldom found among many.

Bishop John [Zlobin] died in a monastery summer retreat (dacha) in South Canaan, Pennsylvania. Evidently, he was removed (the Metropolia wanted to receive more income from Alaska); he ultimately did not please them. Apparently, his last years were not easy ones.... As a monk from the Svyatogorsk Monastery in the south of Russia, he was dreaming of establishing a monastery on Spruce Island, but he couldn't find any suitable people. Bishop Alexey Panteleev (later Archbishop of Omsk) used to live on Spruce Island. He left in the house on Monks' Lagoon some Greek books; apparently he was familiar with the Greek language and loved it. Deacon Basil [Hierodeacon Elias] Shchukin lived on the beach; there remained some kind of buildings of his, cells that belonged to him. Father Macarius Kocybinsky, a native of southern Russia from a family of renowned priests, came from Mount Athos. He had lived at Karoulia on Mount Athos, but fearing communism, he

---

*A famous Russian priest before the Russian Revolution, known for his outstanding sermons.

decided to come to America and to Alaska. He was not able to get along with Father Gerasim, and they were not on friendly terms. Without a doubt Father Macarius had monastic ways and habits and was well read in spiritual literature, but when he arrived in Sitka from New York, by that time he had been carried away with the writings of Bishop Porphyrius Uspensky and *The Pillar and Foundation of the Truth* by Father Paul Florensky. Evidently, his interest toward ascetic monasticism had cooled off within him.

On the same island Father Sergius Irtel* with his novice Alexander Outracht (now Father Seraphim) also labored, but he fell into prelest and ran away.

It remains now in question what really was predicted by the blessed Father Herman, i.e., what would be on Spruce Island, a monastery, or "This place will not remain empty, and another (or others) fleeing the glory of men will live on it," or both.

To Br. Gleb....

Sch. Theodore
[Schema-bishop Theodore (Sergius Irtel)]

---

*The author of this letter, Hieromonk Sergius before tonsure into the schema, is speaking derogatorily about himself as if it were someone else.

Saint Euphrosyne the "Unknown," a contemporary icon.

APPENDIX II

Blessed Euphrosyne

THE BLESSED FOOL-FOR-CHRIST'S sake known as Euphrosyne, buried near the town of Alexin, was born Princess Eudocia of Viazma. As a young lady she graduated from the prestigious Smolny Institute in St. Petersburg, then became a lady-in-waiting in the court of Empress Catherine II. Princess Eudocia was acquainted with a number of other important noblewomen and had the ability to humor and console the Empress in difficult times.

It is not known how long the princess lived in the Imperial Court, but eventually she and two other ladies-in-waiting agreed amongst themselves to leave the world of luxury and high society and live the rest of their lives in ascetic struggle. One day the three noblewomen left their dresses on the shore of a large, deep pond near the imperial palace, to imply that they had drowned, for they wished to put to rest all inquiry into their disappearance. They then dressed in rough peasant shirts and began to wander as pilgrims in voluntary poverty and foolishness for Christ's sake.

Blessed Euphrosyne labored in the stables of the Monastery of St. Theodosius of Totma in Vologda province, and in the prosphora bakery of another monastery. Having mortified her flesh, she embarked upon her life of prayer, asking Metropolitan Plato of Moscow to guard the secret of her identity. The Metropolitan sent her to the Monastery of Serpukhov, where she began to labor as a fool-for-Christ. She eventually settled outside the monastery gates in a tiny hut.

In this little hut she kept cats and three dogs, sleeping with the dogs on the bare floor. When people asked why she allowed dogs to sleep with her, she answered: "I am worse than a dog." Her cell was always dirty and strewn with the leavings of the animals' food. She justified the stench there, saying that it took the place of the perfumes she had so often worn at court. It was an austere life of self-mortification—she wore iron chains, a long, heavy hair shirt, and went barefoot. On her chest was a large brass cross suspended on an iron chain, and she walked around the monastery at night singing spiritual folk songs. She often healed people who came to her with faith by giving them herbs she had gathered.

She was well loved in Serpukhov, but persecutions against her arose, forcing her to move. A noblewoman of the village of Koliupanova in Tula Province, Natalia Alexeevna Protopopova loved her very much, and built Euphrosyne a nice house on her property, into which the blessed one settled her cow, herself moving into a small room in the noblewoman's house, together with chickens, turkeys, cats, dogs and all their progeny. The smell was unbearable to the average man.

Her spiritual heights were hard to comprehend, even for those who wished to do so. Anyone who came to see her might find her snoring amongst the animals, and would unfailingly be greeted by barking dogs.

The blessed one prayed continually with great rapture and ate very little—whatever the dogs left her. She was clairvoyant, healed the sick, and made peace among people in enmity. She often went about to people in neighboring villages, staying with them and helping them in their needs. Knowing in spirit of looming danger, she frequently saved others by her prayers and prayed for souls departing their bodies afar off. She foresaw the invasion of Napoleon even before he came to power in France and described his appearance.

When people came to see her, she would often give them something to eat as a form of prophecy. A turnip or pepper signified woes to come; pancakes meant a death in the family.

Euphrosyne died at the great age of 120 years—a righteous and miraculous repose. One Sunday she came near to the church during Liturgy and shouted that there were two angels in white garments coming out of the church, calling her to themselves, saying "Euphrosynushka, it's time for you to come to us!" She had the same vision three Sundays in a row at the same time during the Liturgy, and on the fourth Sunday, at the end of Liturgy, she quietly and painlessly reposed at 3:00 p.m. on July 3, 1855, her hands crossed upon her chest. Her face shone, and a fragrance filled the room.

Her simple wooden coffin was buried under the Kazan church in Koliupanovo, according to the blessing of Metropolitan Philaret (Drozdov) of Moscow,* who had always revered the ascetic, and conducted spiritual discussions with her. A grave-plate bearing the Metropolitan's name commemorates her forever as "Euphrosyne the Unknown."

People came from all over Russia to visit her grave, where miracles were wrought, for the eldress continued to heal the sick even after her death. Elders from the St. Tikhon of Kaluga Hermitage, located a hundred miles away came to visit her, as well as Elder Gerasim, the builder of the St. Sergius Skete near St. Tikhon's. Thus did God glorify the princess who rejected every comfort and consolation the world had to offer, even her own identity.

---

*Now canonized.

ELDER GERASIM THE SECOND
when he was 40 years old, nurtured in St. Tikhon's Monastery
in the spirit of the Optina Elders.

APPENDIX III

Elder Gerasim the Second (or the Younger) of St. Tikhon of Kaluga Monastery

COMMEMORATED JULY 31 (†1918)

Thirty years after the death of Elder Gerasim the Second, the following account was discovered, written by his sterling disciple and spiritual son from the tonsure, Archimandrite Simeon, whom he sent to America. We include it here in order to preserve it for Elder Gerasim's venerators.

Fr. Gerasim of Spruce Island told me that when he was tonsured he was given the name Gerasim, not only for Gerasim of the Jordan, but also in honor of the two Gerasims of Kaluga, because they were native to Fr. Gerasim's Alexin.

IN 1918, on the 31st of July, during the worst conflagration of the devil's demonic exhalations, by God's will reposed Elder Gerasim (born in 1864), the Superior and founder of the St. Sergius of Radonezh Imperial Skete in Kaluga Province.

The Skete is located six miles from the St. Tikhon Monastery, in which Fr. Gerasim laid his foundation, having entered the monastery at the age of fourteen (in 1878). This beginning was notable in that his elderly mother had brought him to the monastery herself. The great clairvoyant elder, also Fr. Gerasim, received the boy into his own care.

The boy lived in obedience to the elder for nearly fifteen years, taking advantage of the clairvoyant elder's instructions and indications for his self-education. Incidentally, it was said of the boy that he lived with the elder, sleeping under his door on the floor. When the monastics asked the elder: "Why does the little boy sleep there on your floor?" he replied: "It's necessary. A great wise man will come of this Misha."

Because he was a humble and thoughtful novice, he was taken to the hierarchical St. Lawrence Monastery within the city limits of Kaluga at the hierarchical residence. Here he received the tonsure and passed through all the usual steps of ascent for monastics up to hieromonk, granted him by His Eminence Macarius (Troitsky). With the blessing of the Kaluga bishops Fr. Gerasim began his activity of planting ascetic life in the Kaluga diocese, and in a short time founded four monasteries for women, each containing up to 150 sisters. The communities were built in such a way that no debts remained on their properties. Soon Fr. Gerasim embarked upon his own path of ascetic life, six miles from the St. Tikhon Hermitage, settling in a dense pine forest, where he built first an earthen hut; and later, when co-ascetics appeared (twelve novices), he offered them the earthen hut, and built for himself a special thatched enclosure. In two years he built a two-story wooden church on a stone foundation, the lower church dedicated to the Dormition of the Mother of God, and the upper church dedicated to St. Sergius of Radonezh.

This holy work was hindered not only by natural difficulties, which had to be overcome by great and persistent labor, but also by official people. But God's mercy aided the work. To the rescue came—and this is significant—secular educated authorities, in the person of the governor and rector of Kaluga. Permission for the building of the Skete was received through their efforts, and as the skete was founded in memory of the assassinated Grand Prince Sergius Alexandrovich, it was taken under the protection of the Kaluga branch of the Imperial Orthodox Palestinian Society and received the name Imperial St. Sergius Skete. This occurred in 1907. By this time there were already twelve small buildings for brothers, one simple but elegant little building for Grand Duchess Elizabeth Feodorovna, where she would stay when she came there in the summer for a rest, and beyond the wall there were also two guesthouses for pilgrims. Later in the skete were built a school, a house for wayfarers and an almshouse for wounded and injured soldiers. It would be natural to ask how the skete ended up with children, for whom a school was built, and elderly men, for whom was built a wayfarers' home. The children were from the village of Mstikhino, Kaluga region, not far from the skete. But the children and the elderly men were gathered mainly by Elder Gerasim himself during trips he made to collect voluntary gifts to the skete. It would happen that the Elder would go to Tula, to Moscow or even to the villages, and instead of returning with donations or bread, he would bring paupers, cripples, the homeless and orphans, two or three at a time, and thus increase the number of the skete's dependents. The children as well as the paupers were in the care of the Elder himself, and so he himself looked after their order and nourishment. He was under no small burden of care also to preserve peace amongst the elderly men, who had been gathered incidentally and therefore often had arguments. Looking after the children, their education, as well as taking care of the wounded and aged—all this lay upon the novices as an obedience, under the personal observation of the Elder himself.

Thus was the activity of the Elder in the skete, beginning in 1897 up to his blessed repose in 1918. The Elder was short in stature, thin of build, but with strong and enduring health. His conduct with the monks was truly angelic. He never had to punish the guilty, because the monks loved the Elder and submitted to him not out of fear, but out of conscience. Nothing ever went to the diocesan council, because the Elder was able to persuade and re-direct even the guilty ones, so that they would abandon the most deeply rooted and persistent vices and habits. His peace-making and penetrating influence revealed itself not only on people, but on demons. The Elder knew how to influence. It would happen that a simple man would come to the hermitage, and make the sign of the cross carelessly. The Elder would be right there: "I feel sorry for you, dear man," he would say; "what good does it do you to wave your hands? Don't you have a brow on which to place the sign of the cross, or a heart to consecrate, or a shoulder on which to carry the cross of Christ? Cross yourself truly and remember the wounds of Christ on yourself." The man would say: "Forgive me, Father," and begin to cross himself correctly. Secular people, even the highly educated, not excluding the Grand Duchess Elizabeth Feodorovna, would fulfill what Elder Gerasim told them to the letter. They ate baked potatoes when they came to the skete, and stood through the entire services that he instructed them to attend. Peasants surprisingly believed in his prayers, and the demonized came to him for healing. It happened once that five men had to drag a "possessed" woman to him. The demon shouted through the woman: "I don't want to go to the skete—'Geraska' is there, he'll kick me out." They dragged the woman, but Elder Gerasim came out to met them. There was one incident, when a possessed woman was dragged to the guesthouse. Elder Gerasim had never seen that woman. When she began to foment, squirm and shout, Hieromonk Irenarch said: "Father is not here, but I will read the prayer over her." He took his cross and holy water, and went to the guesthouse to read the prayer [of exorcism] over the sick woman. As soon as he came into the room, the woman exclaimed: "Irenarch, this is not your business. Only Geraska can chase me out." The hieromonk was amazed by the power of the demon, that the woman should call him by name, having never seen him. Fr. Gerasim arrived. They told him about the sick woman. He served on the second day a Liturgy for her health. The woman screamed unnaturally during the Liturgy, but when Elder Gerasim came out with the Holy Gifts to commune her, he commanded her to be silent. The woman immediately obeyed. Then he made the sign of the cross over her with a prayer for the forgiveness of sins and served her right away. After Liturgy he served a moleben to St. Sergius of Radonezh with an Akathist to the Mother of God, and dismissed the woman. She felt perfectly healthy. She began to thank the elder right away, saying: "Thank you, Father. You have healed me." But the Elder said that he was not worthy of this gratitude, for it was the Mother of God who had healed her.

Elder Gerasim's repose was blessed. Our Elder departed, and he was not buried for nine days. There were no signs of decay discovered on his body. There was not even a smell from the dead body. The reason they did not bury him for so long is not hard to discern: apparently the monastics did not hurry to commit his body to the earth, for they believed in the Elder's sanctity and wanted to challenge the spreading unbelief and bolshevik aggression against holy relics. They wanted to show that even now it is possible to see with one's own eyes the truth of faith in incorrupt relics, as is revealed even now by the remains of those righteous ones who pleased God.

The Elder died in the fifty-fifth year of his life. He began to bear the name of "Elder" according to the common voice of the monastics, even from the time the skete was being founded, although one could not say that he had the appearance of an old man.*

---

*From *Russky Palomnik*, No. 16, 1997, pp. 132-134.

Funeral procession of Fr. Gerasim on Spruce Island, led by Bishop Theodosius of Sitka (now Metropolitan of the OCA). The cross is the one planted by Fr. Gerasim thirty-two years before on the site of his own grave.

APPENDIX IV

The Death of Father Gerasim

Below are presented two letters written by Gene Sundberg, to whom Fr. Gerasim was Godfather and nurturer of his whole family.

LETTER ONE
October 25, 1965

Dear Gleb,

This is to inform you that my old and dear friend Father Gerasim died on October 12 at the Kodiak Borough Hospital, and was buried at his beloved Monks' Lagoon, on October 15, 1969. You may have already heard about it, but I felt I should write you myself.

I shall try to relate to you our association over the past four or five years. I'm sorry I haven't done this sooner, as you did ask about him once or twice over these years.

Father Gerasim was very much involved during the earthquake and tidal wave, having almost lost his life during the wave. He was in the water up to his neck and, as he said afterward, was prepared to go then. He was in Ouzinkie at this time. After this happened he seemed to get sick more frequently—the people of the village called for me twice, fearing that he was going to die. He apparently had two heart attacks, as later electrocardiographs would show. So, in September of 1965, after setting up a small house on my property adjacent to my home, I brought him to Kodiak, to the hospital for a check-up and to rest comfortably for as long as he wanted. It was really nice to have him this close to us. I especially enjoyed it because this gave him a good chance to come to love my sons or, I should say, for them to love him as I and my father, and my father's father before him had. With my sons, it made four generations of Sundbergs he came into close contact with.

We enjoyed him, loved him and had fun with him for about three of the four years; but then he grew old, and his legs really began to give out. His mind began to wander back to his homeland and his earlier life in the Kodiak Island group. He became senile, and at many times didn't know us anymore. This was an especially hard time for us, because not only would he not know us, but would be afraid of us, or anybody for that matter. He began to huddle inside himself. He became so forgetful that the only thought left in his mind was to get to Monks' Lagoon and Father Herman. During this period we prayed many times for God to take him and spare him the agony he must have been going through. He then started wandering at night, and it was at this point that we put him in the hospital and began looking for a nursing home. After much negotiating we were able to keep him in a room at the Kodiak Hospital set aside for patients of Medi-Care. This was in June of this year. He had many good days there, and of course some bad. We were naturally his constant visitors. They put him on a new tranquilizer for elderly people suffering from over-anxiety, and he seemed to be back to normal. We called it a miracle drug, but this just proved to be the calm before the storm. Shortly afterward he just quieted down, would hardly talk and just sat and stared at the walls all day long, even when I would come and visit. About the first week in October the doctor informed me that Father Gerasim had developed double pneumonia. The doctors and nurses tried to do everything in their power to save him, but to no avail. He continued to worsen. I called my two sisters, Marylin from Anchorage and Glenace from Lake Tahoe, whom he dearly loved. He did recognize Glenace and said her name, which was really something, because I hadn't heard him say a word for over a week. We visited him morning, noon and night during the last few days. And finally on

Sunday, October 12, a beautiful sunny day when Father Targansky gave him his usual Sunday Communion, we noticed he was in extremely bad condition. At 10:15 that night the hospital called and Glenace and I went, said our good byes to him and watched the priest give him the last Sacrament of Extreme Unction. Father Gerasim requested it and hung on till the last prayer, and when it was finished, he just peacefully left us. I keep saying this—but it was so beautiful, I know I smiled. I certainly hope I'm lucky enough to go like that, because there was no pain, no strain, no effort, no change of expression or outcries. Just beautiful.

Arrangements were then made for the funeral and getting the body to Monks' Lagoon. The Bishop of Alaska, Theodosius, came to Kodiak for the services, but I had a time getting a boat to take him to Monks' Lagoon. It's that time of year for our easterly and north-easterlies, and I believe you know what that means. The swells are so big that boats are unable to get into the bay. According to most skippers of the boats, our only chance was to take the body to Pestrikoff Beach and walk him in the three miles to his house. The day of the funeral we would decide if it was safe or not. So, on October 15, 1969, the service started at 9 a.m. and continued till about 1:30. The sea was still rough, but the boat captains felt we could make it, so we carried Father Gerasim to a waiting boat and took him home. After a fairly rough trip, we landed at Pestrikoff Beach and began what was the most exhilarating experience I have ever had.

It was really something to see all the people that came to see him home. The boys of Ouzinkie came to clear a path wide enough for the casket and pallbearers, and to put down logs across the creeks and bad swampy areas. About a hundred men, women and children made the trek. The pallbearers would change every few minutes, and there were enough of them that we would never really get tired. There were many tough spots to cross and get over, but not once did the caravan of people, bent on getting Father Gerasim home to rest, falter or stop on the trail. After a two-hour walk we arrived at the spot he had chosen for himself thirty-two years ago: the cross marker in his front yard. There, after a short service, he was laid to rest in the place he loved best and *near* the one he loved best, his Father Herman. The hard work getting him there had been worth it. The women of Ouzinkie had perok and pies, coffee and tea, waiting for us. The air was filled with the same joyful feeling we used to have with Father Gerasim and *our tea parties* outside his cabin. It was a good feeling for me—to know that he was at complete rest now. Some people said the birds began to sing as if welcoming him back home. Others said there were sweet fragrances, and even some said they felt as though Father Herman was watching us. I believe them all. It had to be. It just had to be that way. He was home, with everything he loved around him.

And so we left him to return home full of the fantastic memories of the day.

His death and burial was somewhat compared to Father Herman's, in that there weren't enough priests to bury him, and so the natives whom he taught and loved carried him to his resting place. The sea was stormy too, but not enough to keep us away.

Many people since then have said to me, what a shame he couldn't see Father Herman's canonization, and I quickly reply, using Father Targansky's words: "Father Gerasim is with Father Herman now, and together they will both watch and be happy." That's true.

Gleb, I've gone on and on here. It's getting late, but I did want to relate to you of our relationship and how happy I am that I was privileged to be able to repay him a little for taking such good care of four generations of just *friends.*

Sincerely,
Gene Sundberg
(A life-long friend to Father Gerasim)

P.S. Thank you for sending *The Orthodox Word* to him all these years. Would you please continue to send them in my name? We all enjoy it very much, especially the parts on Father Herman. G.S.

Also, a "Father Herman Canonization Fund" has been started at the Kodiak Russian Orthodox Church.

LETTER TWO
November 20, 1969

Dear Gleb,

I have just returned home from church services for Father Gerasim—his forty days since death. I have had your letter sitting out on our bulletin board so I wouldn't forget to write to you, but it seems I keep putting it off. I seem to have this trouble. The Bishop's secretary is also asking me to get busy on a project I agreed to do, but with my work in the grocery business, I find I must squeeze things in. There should just be about 28 hours in a day.

To answer your questions: Father Gerasim was buried at a spot about seventy-five feet from his bedroom window, to the east of his house, approximately in the center of the clearing. He set in a cross to mark the site that he wished to be buried thirty-two years ago. After he died, the Bishop asked that we have the cross brought over to Kodiak for the funeral procession, so the boys from Ouzinkie sent it over. Although it was quite heavy and water-logged, it was not rotten as most woods, especially fir, will get when sunk into the ground. Also, it is a 10-foot-high cross and was sunk into the ground only 14 inches, and yet it never fell over from the heavy snows or the high winds. I send to you a photograph to show you the location where he was buried, also notice the high-water mark on the cross. I thought it was very ironic.

My wife has compiled a book about Father Gerasim, and any of the pictures I send [are] to come from it, so I cannot stress too greatly the importance of them. I will expect them back as soon as you can make copies of them.

Birthday—November 9, 1888, in the village of Alexin, province or state of Tula, Russia.

In 1916 he came to Sitka, Alaska, on November 8th, under Bishop Philip.

As for the icon of St. Seraphim, I do not feel I am in the position to offer any of his holy possessions, as I believe they are the properties of the church. Therefore, I ask that you contact Bishop Theodosius, to whom I have turned over his personal church items. I would have loved that icon, too, as I know how dearly he loved it, but I just could not.

I, personally, have no holy object of his other than his letters or his handwork, which to us are treasures which we won't part with.

As far as I know, Bishop Theodosius has no one coming to take Father Gerasim's place, but I am sure someone must come if Father Herman is to become a saint. I feel Monks' Lagoon will become a shrine, and with the many more visitors that will come, someone will have to protect those holy items that are there.

I am also sure that once the services of sainthood are performed and someone is at Monks' Lagoon to watch over everything, the relics of Father Herman will be taken back to where they belong. I think I would have a feeling of robbing a grave to leave them here, and I would do all in my power to see that they were returned. I would imagine you feel the same way.

Gleb, I have tried to answer all of your questions, and now I would like you to answer one for me. In all the years I have known Father Gerasim, I have known that he was a member of another part of the Russian Church other than the Kodiak Church, that is: as I understand, the Russian Church in exile, to return to Russia, or something like that. I never have been able to get a clear picture of just what the Russian Church is doing to itself in this country. Are there three different factions, and if so, are they going to be able to work together on this great event of Father Herman's canonization and make it the greatest event in the church's history in this country; or stay in a state of disunity and hurt themselves further? I would like

Church on the Little Afognak in 1912,
just prior to Fr. Gerasim's assignment to Afognak.

to feel that they can work together; after all, isn't that what religion is all about????

Our local paper is coming out with a pamphlet on Father. I will send you a copy as soon as it comes out.

Sincerely yours,
Gene Sundberg

Please let me know if I can be of more help to you.

Please accept this calendar of my place of work. I have been made general manager of this beautiful store. Notice the change in Kodiak. The tidal wave of 1964, of course, wiped out the old downtown section.

ADMIRAL BARON FERDINAND P. WRANGELL.
A family portrait sent to our Brotherhood by
his great-grandson from Estonia.

APPENDIX V

East Spruce Island to be New Valaam

A Deed from Russia to American Monasticism

COVER LETTER FROM THE TRANSLATOR:

19 September 1983

Dear Abbot Herman:

In reply to your letter of 29 August, I enclose:

1) a photocopy of the document #354 which I mention in *The Russian Orthodox Religious Mission in America, 1794-1837,* p. 178. I was reviewing there the information provided in the correspondence of the governors of the Russian-American Company. In this case it was Baron Wrangell (1830-1835) who wrote this [document] while on a visit to Kodiak, as an instruction to the local office.

2) a translation of the above document (which is like a deed to that portion of the island!).

With best wishes,
Richard A. Pierce
Department of History
Queens University
Kingston, Canada

Correspondence, Governors of Russian America, Communications sent, 1831, 365a-357a

1831, June 18. #354 Proposal, to Kodiak Office

By personal inspection I have ascertained that Father Herman's enterprise on Spruce Island can be a nursery (that is, can help promote gardening) for all of Kodiak—and not only gardening but in the course of time, and with constant effort, refinement of manners. In view of that side of this enterprise, I order the following with regard to it, which I purpose that this office carry out, namely:

1) This establishment will henceforth be called New Valaam and that name will be used in correspondence.

2) The entire east cape of the island, where the gardens are now located, will be considered as belonging to this enterprise, and Aleuts, Russians and creoles will not be allowed to settle in New Valam without Father Herman's permission.

3) A harbor will be built at company expense.

4) If any Aleuts, creoles or Russians, with Father Herman's permission, wish to settle in New Valaam, give permission for that, but no one is to settle there without knowledge of the office. Aleuts who owe to the company, and any who have not yet served the company will not be allowed in New Valaam, and it will be more preferable to permit those Aleuts, Russians and creoles who have finished their lawful period of service to move there, along with minor orphans, widows, and elderly persons with families.

5) Without Father Herman's consent no one will be settled (elsewhere) and no one will be taken from New Valaam into company service, and if there is a legal need for any of the inhabitants of Valaam to enter in temporary service of the company, the office will please take the matter up with Father Herman, who will never without satisfactory reason keep anyone from carrying out company obligations.

Commemoration postage stamp from Russia today, 1997,
featuring a portrait of Baron Ferdinand P. Wrangell.
"Explorers of Russian Territories, 1829-1835."

6) If for improvement of the enterprise cattle are needed, agricultural tools and the like, on request of Father Herman, issue the money for such needs without interest, and in general by all means aid the enterprise and satisfy the useful and lawful requests of Father Herman.

[Baron Ferdinand P. Wrangell,
Governor of the Russian-American Company]

The St. Herman Brotherhood in 1988, one thousand years since
the Baptism of Russia, in front of the church of St. Herman of
Alaska—newly built by the brothers themselves—in Platina.

APPENDIX VI

Fr. Gerasim's Brotherhood

ALTHOUGH THE LETTERS of Fr. Gerasim to me do not show any
theological or literary pretensions, they are nevertheless quite indicative
of the attitude towards many Church matters typical of many like Fr.
Gerasim who carried the burden of Orthodox Christianity in the 20th
century. He wrote these letters to a seminary fledgling who was just
beginning his ecclesiastical career in these harsh times for traditional
Orthodox Christianity at the end of the 20th century. He felt that his
ecclesiastical orientation must be properly understood, and he attempted to transmit it to his brothers who cared to follow him. His
position was simple: he accepted all Orthodox Churches in the New
World, outside of their natural countries of origin. And he objected to
any innovations and departures from that Orthodoxy in which he was
formed and to which he was loyal until his death. It is fair to tell now
the truth of Fr. Gerasim's attitude to the church divisions, which are
painfully present in America and outside of it.

As to the Greek Church, he objected to the spirit of renovationism,
ecumenism and Greek chauvinism, and the hierarchs' participation in
Masonic lodges; but of course he revered Byzantium.

The Moscow Patriarchate was to him a legitimate Church, but he
vehemently objected to Sergianism while also understanding that the
Church in Russia was in captivity. He objected to the Red hierarchs
who were denying the persecution of religion in Russia throughout the
whole world while enjoying Western freedom.

He objected to the spineless and cunning attitude in the American Metropolia dominant in Alaska, accusing their bishops of harshness, lack of pastoral zeal, small-mindedness, disdain towards old traditions and Russian monarchy, and illegitimate usurpation of power, but he did not deny their apostolic succession. He could not tolerate the "New" Autocephaly coming from a soviet concordat through Metropolitan Nicodemus, chief Sergianist and ecumenist of the day (who even died in Rome at the feet of the Pope). When in 1969 Bishops Theodosius and Juvenal visited Fr. Gerasim in his Kodiak bungalow and told him of the Autocephaly (OCA foundation), he literally kicked the bishops off his porch, and they tumbled down, which was seen by neighbors.

The Russian Church Outside of Russia, wherein lay his sympathies, he criticized for its extremism and self-righteousness to the extent of denying grace in other jurisdictions. He saw in this the roots of Old Believerism. His severe criticism was best expressed in his correspondence with and irritation towards Archimandrite Constantine of Jordanville.

He knew very well that the cause of the "New Calendar" in Greece and Renovationism in the 20th century in the Orthodox Church was "given flesh" only thanks to communist indoctrination; even Patriarch Tikhon was at one time tempted by this.

His lamentations mostly centered upon the all-encompassing march of Western Christendom's Apostasy, since most of the Orthodox Churches, even if they denied such influence, did nothing to defend traditional Orthodoxy.

As for the Brotherhood he founded, he felt that their sacred duty was to adhere to the above-mentioned convictions and attitudes which he held. The Brotherhood in return, so well expressed by Fr. Seraphim Rose, consciously upheld their founder's positions, promoting them widely in their publications throughout the world and, consequently, receiving abuse from the "powerful of this world" who up to today grumble against them.

This Brotherhood grew slowly, as the path they chose was as thorny as that of their founders. During his lifetime Fr. Gerasim did not reach the English-speaking world in his stand for Orthodoxy, yet through his solitary stand he spoke adequately enough for oppressed and suffering traditional Orthodoxy. Ten years after I last saw him I wrote my impressions of him for an article in our magazine, *The Orthodox Word*. Fr. Gerasim poured out many prayers at the grave and relics of St. Herman for this magazine.

***

I visited Fr. Gerasim on Spruce Island near Kodiak, Alaska, when he had already had twenty-five years of desert dwelling and was worn out from the unjust suffering inflicted on him for his refusal to adjust himself to church politics; this struggle also undermined his spiritual strength. He lived in a small hut 500 steps from the roaring ocean shore in an extremely thick spruce forest. So dense is this northern jungle that one cannot walk through it save on the laid-out paths. Farther on in the thicket is the chapel built in 1894 over the grave of St. Herman.

His cell, which he built himself, had a little annex, his bedroom, where he conducted his prayer-rule, and a low closet for firewood near his stove. Everything was neat and orderly to perfection: freshly painted and often-swept floors, quilted rugs, lace curtains and a bedspread over a hard-board bed, and many inexpensive icons with a number of hanging lamps. I immediately recognized that his excessive tidiness was a means of keeping sanity in this intense loneliness and the overwhelming growth of the wilderness. The coziness was for the sake of warmth but not comfort, which is deadly for a Christian everywhere and always.

Like St. Herman, he occasionally had to go to take care of his Aleut flock, who lived at the other end of this impenetrable island, but he preferred to stay permanently in his beloved hermitage, caring for St. Herman's grave. There he unfailingly performed all the monastic church services, praying alone for the world, lost in the denseness of the Alaskan wilds.

During the Dormition fast he served akathists in his cell every day at 5:00 p.m. and commemorated *all* the people he had met in his life. The lists were endless, and so were his tears. I was shaken to the depths of my soul at that prayer. I was caught up in the fervency of his pleading, imploring prayer, and I could not help but weep my heart out, as I never had before or after. But the tears were not tears of sorrow, but of some sweet, unexplainable contrition of heart. There before me, in the commemoration of his friends, passed the whole panorama of his life, for I recognized the names of his parents, monks, bishops, Athonites, fellow laborers in the vineyard of Christ in Alaska, and endless names of his spiritual children whom he had baptized, married, and then sung burial services for—many of them lost in the cold waters of the stormy ocean.

About this I wrote then in my journal the following: "I think that for his hard life on Spruce Island, the Lord, through the prayers of Fr. Herman, strengthens him and manifests him as a true ascetic. I say it because of the following personal experience I had, which, however, could be interpreted in various ways.

"The very first day of my arrival, that is on the eve of the Transfiguration, after Divine Liturgy, a meal and a pannikhida in the chapel over the grave of Fr. Herman, Fr. Gerasim said to me with an air of embarrassment, prefacing it with his constantly repeated, favorite expression 'Forgive me' (in Russian *prosteete*, which he stresses with the prolonged sound 'EE'): 'Forgive me; but during Dormition Fast I have the habit of reading the Akathist to the Theotokos every day from the Prayer Book and commemorating those on my list of commemorations.'

"I was also a bit embarrassed with his embarrassment and in turn begged his forgiveness for my intrusion, but wanted very much to at least be present at his prayers. And he began to pray in his tiny bedroom. (This bedroom was where I slept while he, giving me his bed, slept in his main cell on a sofa.) His bed consisted of simple hard boards but was covered with elaborate lace pillow coverings with old-fashioned

Fr. Gerasim in his Afognak days, in the late 1920's,
in his white Paschal cassock so typical of him.

bows, as I had seen in Russian homes in my childhood. But I understood this as his longing for his homelife in Russia, as well as his love for neatness and cleanliness.

"He stood at an analogion (near an old, large life-size oil painting-icon of St. Seraphim of Sarov) and behind him I stood near the door, just a few steps from him. A pure, heartfelt prayer began to flow out of him with exclamations—the fervent pleas of an old man which came straight out of a living soul. I was singing along at the refrains.

"But after the akathist, he began to commemorate both the living and the dead—all whomever he knew during his 73-year-old life. And here I, it seemed without any apparent reason, began to weep with repentant tears. My whole soul, it seemed to me, sobbed not from sorrow but from some spiritual joy, which is impossible to describe or even understand. I saw before me a man sincerely praying and remembering people with such great warmth; a man forgotten and abandoned by the whole world, imploring God to have pity on it, a man in the midst of this impenetrable wilderness, faraway in this northern jungle. All this was too much for my poor soul. And I wept and sobbed....

"What I then felt, listening to his prayer, I believe was a breath of the Holy Spirit touching my evil and sinful soul! And he, as if oblivious to my presence, went on and on. He prayed and I wept."

Having finished this prayer, as if nothing had happened he was cheerful again, offering me tea and salmon pie of his own baking; and only the starry sky far above the gigantic dark spruces bore witness to the length of his standing before God. But my heart felt unusually light, and a burning inspiration transfigured all my being.

He told me much during my unforgettable stay with him, about his Kaluga childhood and the Holy Russia he bore in his loving heart, about the Optina Elders, his Athonite period, and the early days of apostolic labors in Alaska. He spoke with sobriety and truth and warm sincerity: about the miracles of Saints Herman and Seraphim that he had seen with his own eyes, and his bitter years of persecution. As his "leitmotif" he frequently returned to his deep sorrow: "Love for God is leaving this planet. Love for Christ is evaporating from the face of this earth."

His standard was basic Christianity of the heart. He was a genuine transmitter of the authentic experience of Orthodox Russia, placed in the context of 20th-century America, and yet so few valued him, or simply misunderstood him. Most of the clergy who were in contact with him were not guarding the age-old Byzantine world view as he was, but were men of a "party" mentality who despised him for his straightforwardness. He knew the truth better; he knew that Orthodox truth ever since the Soviet Revolution was destined to be persecuted and thus suffer belittlement or various forms of distortion. He knew well the spirit of "renovationists." Yet he also knew well that the Truth will make men free, and his conscience commanded him to speak out—and so he spoke, eloquently, to the point, with humbleness of heart, uncomplicated and brief. While Archimandrite Gerasim is not considered a theologian by those whose concept of theology requires learned homilies and advanced degrees, he is indeed a theologian in the true and ancient sense of the word—one who knows God. He knew God not simply through book-knowledge, but by a life of true Christian struggle and prayer. It is precisely this *living* Christianity which ignites the heart and sheds the light of Christ into the darkness of the world.

The days were long and warm, late in August. We took walks together, and he showed me spots of unbelievably abundant ripe boysenberries. I ate to satiety, but he only picked berries and made a pie for me. There he used to meet bears and other wild animals. The craggy shores abounded with multicolored wildflowers, and the constant flow of his tales of the saints of old and Russian ascetics involuntarily transported my imagination to St. Herman's Valaam or Fr. Gerasim's beloved Mt. Athos, where he knew and corresponded with many righteous slaves of God.

There also, at the grave of St. Herman, my spiritual life was transformed and a dedication to the cause of St. Herman was born. We

Fr. Gerasim on the shore of Monks' Lagoon, just as he looked when
I saw him for the last time, in tears saying to me, when I asked why the tears:
"I hate parting, saying goodbyes. Just think, we shall never meet again
in this world.... I hope to see you in the other."

spent together the hundredth anniversary of the canonization of St. Tikhon of Zadonsk in solemn all-night vigil. I read to him my seminary thesis on this Saint, which in the tenderness of his heart brought tears to his eyes.

I covered many important subjects with him, and I was exposed to a new, indispensable dimension which my seminary education had not covered: what America and our 20th-century world needs is to have a *living link* with the universal Apostolic Tradition, a link which no books or learned lectures can give; this is, as it were, the mystical aspect of apostolic succession.

When I was leaving him, an abandoned, even despised old man standing there in tears alone on the shore of Monks' Lagoon, I knew then that I had beheld, contrary to my expectation, a spiritual giant who breathed into me a *life of decision,* a resolve for a living continuation of St. Herman's work for the glory of God in His Orthodox Church, and that, with God's help, *nothing* could take this away from me.

Upon the prayers of Fr. Gerasim our Brotherhood became not only outspoken defenders of the positions he held, but also disseminators of the now rare, beautiful, "inner world" he loved, through their translation and publication. It was this "better part" (cf. Lk. 10:42), this "Living Tradition" of the essence of Christianity that is such a stumbling block to the worldly "wise and prudent," so easy to miss, and yet so precious, that gave Fr. Gerasim the strength to endure in the path God had appointed for him to tread.

Well done, thou good and faithful servant: thou has been faithful over a few things, I will make thee ruler over many things: enter thou into the joy of thy Lord (Matt. 25:21, 23).

Abbot Herman
January 21/February 3, 1998
St. Maximus the Confessor

INDEX

INDEX

239

INDEX